Geoff Hamilton's
Gardener's
Challenge

Written in collaboration with
Marion and Paddy Lightfoot

Kingfisher Books

Kingfisher Books, Grisewood & Dempsey Ltd, Elsley House, 24–30 Great Titchfield Street, London W1P 7AD

First published in 1993 by Kingfisher Books

10 9 8 7 6 5 4 3 2 1

BRITISH LIBRARY CATALOGUING IN PUBLICATION DATA
A catalogue record for this book is available from the British Library

ISBN 1-85697-050-7

Senior Editor: Stuart Cooper
Assistant Editor: Janice Lacock
Design: Kelly Flynn
Cover: Smiljka Surla
Picture Research: Elaine Willis

Phototypeset by Southern Positives and Negatives (SPAN), Lingfield, Surrey
Printed in Italy

ACKNOWLEDEGEMENTS

The publishers would like to thank the following artists for their contribution to this book:

Jonathan Adams, Sarah De Ath, Isobel Balakrishnan, Norma Birgin, Richard Bonson, Wendy Bramall, Terry Callcut, Peter Chesterton, John Davis, Colin Emberson, Will Giles, Sandra Pond, George Thompson

The publishers also wish to thank the following for supplying photographs for this book:

Cover: clockwise from left Stephen Hamilton, Zefa, Zefa, Harry Smith, Harry Smith

Page 4, 77 Stephen Hamilton; 5, 47, 95, 113 Timothy Woodcock; 7, 9 (right), 33 (right), 39, 45 (bottom left), 57 (bottom), 63 (right), 74, 87 (right), 93 (right), 111, 117 (left) Paul Forrester; 10 (left) Coke Estates Ltd; 10 (right), 58 (left), 64 (right) Royal Horticultural Society; 12 (top), 14 (left), 17, 20, 21, 23, 24 (left), 25, 31 (left), 32, 37, 38, 45 (top left), 49, 51 53, 55, 57 (top), 62, 67, 69, 71, 75, 79, 81, 83, 86, 87 (left), 99, 101, 107, 109, 110, 114, 116 (left), 118, 120, 122, 123, 124 (left) Harry Smith; 16 (left) Helene Rogers; 16 (right), 22 (right), 28 (left), 34 (right), 52 (right), 70 (left), 76 (right), 94 (left), 106 (bottom), 112 (bottom) Mansell Collection; 18 (bottom), 48 (top), 102 (top), 103 A-Z Botanical Collection; 22 (top left) Patrick Thurston; 22 (bottom left), 70 (top), 112 (top) Anthea Beszant; 28 (right), 82 (right) Liz Eddison; 29, 34 (left), 100, 106 (middle) Rod Edwards; 40 (left) Historic Royal Palaces Crown Copyright (left); 40 Victoria & Albert Museum (right); 46 Allan Ridsdale; 52 (left), 65 Patricia Winter; 58 (right), 88 (left) Neil Campbell-Sharp; 59 Derbyshire Countryside Ltd; 64 (left) Ian Brodie; 76 (left), 82 (left) Wales Tourist Board; 88 (bottom) Heather Angel; 90 (bottom) Pat Brindley; 94 (left) Jeff Waldock; 106 (top) Eye Ubiquitous; 124 (right) Royal Botanic Gardens, Kew

All other photographs by Brian Davis

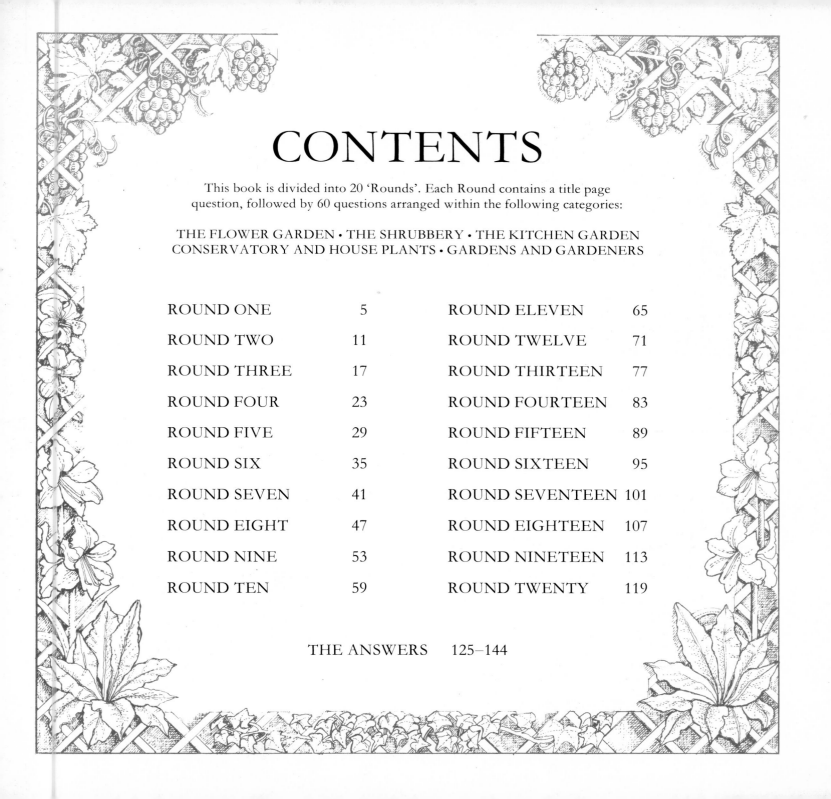

CONTENTS

This book is divided into 20 'Rounds'. Each Round contains a title page
question, followed by 60 questions arranged within the following categories:

THE FLOWER GARDEN · THE SHRUBBERY · THE KITCHEN GARDEN
CONSERVATORY AND HOUSE PLANTS · GARDENS AND GARDENERS

INTRODUCTION

If you want to know everything about gardening your best bet is to become a Buddhist. You'd certainly need to be reincarnated at least half-a-dozen times to learn it all! The noble art of horticulture is such an immensely wide subject that no-one, however experienced and however much involved, could possibly assimilate all that knowledge in one lifetime.

I've been involved in horticulture all my life and I still learn something new every day. I suppose that's one of the fascinations.

Despite that, or perhaps because of it, gardeners are always eager to show off their knowledge and to share it with others. Oh, certainly, there's sometimes an element of one-upmanship in it. We've all met the 'plantsmen' who vist your garden and try to prove their horticultural superiority with something like "I see your *Pterocarya fraxinifolia dumosa* is suffering somewhat. A little monosodium glutamate deficiency perhaps". But, on the other side of the coin, you only have to work on an allotment for a week or two to experience real kindness and comradeship from older, more experienced gardeners eager to help.

So I hope you'll get a lot of fun out of our *Challenge* and that you learn something too. Having said that, one of the great problems of my job is that we British are such a very good race of gardeners. There are so many specialists about who have become engrossed in growing perhaps dahlias or chrysanths or alpines and have been doing so for years. In that time they've probably assimilated such a wealth of knowledge of their particular subject that I know I take my life in my hands every time I even attempt to give advice!

The *Challenge* consists of twenty 'Rounds', each divided into five separate subjects with many of the questions illustrated. In each round you'll find some easy questions and some really quite difficult ones, so don't expect to get full marks in any of them.

Gardening techniques have, in the main, been avoided because we all have our own particular ways of doing things. Instead, this is a quiz about gardening fact, from coir to kiwi-fruit, fuchsias to Floriade and junipers to Jekyll.

As you will know, gardeners can't completely avoid botanical names, though, since the botanists are forever changing them, that does present something of a problem. At the time of writing, I'm pretty sure they're all up to date.

I see the *Challenge* as not just an enjoyable way to learn more about our fascinating pastime at home but hopefully as a source of entertainment for garden clubs and societies too.

So I've thrown down the gardening glove. I hope you will pick it up and that you'll accept the *Challenge* in the spirit in which it's intended. Have a lot of fun and learn a bit along the way, and this little book will have done its job. I hope you enjoy it.

ROUND ONE

Built in 1851 by Sir Charles Barry, the house once belonged to the Astors and is now administered by the National Trust as a hotel. The 375 acres of garden and woodland include a magnificent parterre, a water garden (pictured here), and a yew walk leading down to the Thames. What country estate is being described?

6 Formerly known as *Funkia*, this hardy, herbaceous plant is grown for its foliage and trumpet-like flowers, and is suitable for shady borders and waterside planting. By what generic name is it now known?

7 Which of the following terms is used to describe a plant that flowers and dies in the second season after germination, producing only its stems, roots and leaves in the first season?
(a) Annual (b) Biennial (c) Perennial

8 What is the common name of the hardy, quick-growing annual *Limnanthes douglasii*, a name the plant acquired from its resemblance to a popular breakfast food?

1 What is the correct generic name for the hardy perennial commonly know as the Day Lily (pictured above)?
(a) *Helxine* (b) *Heliopsis* (c) *Hemerocallis*

2 Do the species *Pieris, Pernettya* and *Philesia* require acid or alkaline soil conditions?

9 Two of the species of *Allium* listed below would be found in the vegetable garden. Which is the odd one out, grown mainly for its ornamental flowers?
(a) *A. moly* (b) *A. porrum*
(c) *A. sativum*

3 A native of southeast Europe, the hardy perennial *Alchemilla* produces intricately branched heads of star-shaped yellow-green flowers, making it a favourite with flower arrangers. What is its common name?

10 The hardy perennial *Acanthus* (shown right) has deeply lobed leaves and tall spikes of mauve and white bracts. What is its common name?

4 In a flower, what name is given to the part of the stamen on which pollen is borne?

5 Approximately how many species make up the *Anemone* genus (shown left) of hardy herbaceous perennials?
(a) 12 (b) 60 (c) 150

11 In a botanical name, what does the word *vulgare* mean?

12 Dog, Marsh and Sweet are the prefixes for three of the ten species of which British hedgerow and woodland flower?

HYDRANGEA

1 These attractive flowering shrubs (pictured left) belong to a genus of around 80 deciduous or evergreen species from China and Japan that are divided into two distinct groups. One is known as Lacecap; what is the other?

2 The half-hardy wall shrub *Cytisus battandieri* differs from other members of the broom family in its leaf shape and in what other non-visual way?

3 Which of the three species listed below does not produce catkins?
(a) Grey Alder (b) Paper Birch (c) Common Beech

4 *Hebe* is a genus of around 100 species of half-hardy shrubs grown for their decorative flowers and foliage. In what other genus, which is named after a saint, were *Hebes* formerly included?

5 To which genus of around 200 shrubs does the spring-flowering, deciduous plant with the common name of Snowball Tree belong?
(a) *Viburnum* (b) *Daphne*
(c) *Deutzia*

6 The Japanese Maple bears attractive, lobed leaves (shown right) which have beautiful autumn colours. What word is used to describe the shape of these leaves, a word which is hinted at in the tree's botanical name?

7 It is usual to cut back *Cornus* and *Eucalyptus* to near ground level each year in order to encourage vigorous shoots for ornamental purposes. What is this practice called?

8 The evergreen shrub *Cistus* or Rock Rose (pictured right) is also known by which other common name, reflecting its Mediterranean origin?
(a) Flame Rose (b) Sun Rose (c) Spanish Rose

9 *Sequoiadendron giganteum* (shown left) has several common names, but which of the following is not applicable?
(a) Giant Redwood (b) Big Tree (c) Dawn Redwood

10 *Clematis* species are among the most popular climbers and are ideal for walls, trellises or poles. Are they self-clinging or twining climbers?

11 What essential step must be taken when planting *Aucuba japonica* or Spotted Laurel to ensure the production of bright scarlet berries?

12 Give one of the two most often used common names of the deciduous shrub *Campsis*, reflecting the shape of its flowers and its growth habit.

1 There are several forms of kale, but which is the type (pictured right) with varieties called 'Spurt' and 'Dwarf Green'?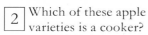

2 Which of these apple varieties is a cooker?
(a) 'Ellison's Orange'
(b) 'James Grieve'
(c) 'Grenadier'

3 Which hardy, deciduous, early-flowering, self-fertilizing tree, originating in China and best grown in this country fan-trained against a warm-sheltered wall, includes the popular variety called 'Moor Park'?

4 What is the popular name given to the fungal disease *Taphrina deformans*, which shows as masses of white spores on the surface of red, swollen leaves and is a common affliction of almonds, cherries, nectarines, peaches (pictured left) and other ornamental members of the *Prunus* genus?

5 Courgettes are nothing more than immature marrows, but why is it essential that all the fruit are cut at the small courgette size and that none should be allowed to mature into marrows?

6 The mid-season variety 'Snowstar' is a popular choice for the vegetable and fruit show, but under what heading would it be exhibited?

7 In grafting, what name is given to the shoot or part of the shoot of one plant that is united with the rootstock of another in order to form a new plant?

8 Which of the following French Bean varieties is a climber rather than a bush type?
(a) 'Tendergreen' (b) 'Blue Lake' (c) 'Radar'

9 What is the common name of the fungal disease that causes brown speckles to appear on the foliage of Broad Bean plants in June or July, or in December or January in over-wintered plants?

10 Match the following types of lettuce with the appropriate varieties:
(i) Loose-leaf (ii) Cos (iii) Crisphead
(a) 'Little Gem' (b) 'Salad Bowl' (c) 'Saladin'

11 At approximately what age would you expect an apricot tree to bear its first fruit?
(a) Two years (b) Four years (c) Six years

12 The candied stems of this herb (shown below) are used in cake and trifle decoration, while its fresh or dried leaves may be infused to make tea. What is it?

1 *Lapageria rosea* (pictured left), which is the only species in its genus, will flower almost all year round if grown in a warm conservatory. What is its common name, reflecting its country of origin?

2 Match the following three genera with the appropriate plant family:
(i) *Vanda* (ii) *Cereus*
(iii) *Adiantum*
(a) Fern (b) Orchid
(c) Cactus

3 The *Nerine* originates in South Africa and bears umbels on two-inch (five centimetre) stems. What are umbels?

4 What unusual feature of *Mimosa pudica* gives rise to its common name of Sensitive Plant?

5 The Iron Cross Begonia (shown left) is a popular house plant grown for its distintive, boldly patterned foliage. Which of the following food storage organs does it have?
(a) Corm (b) Tuber
(c) Rhizome

6 *Nertera*, popularly called Bead Plant or Coral Moss, is a decorative, creeping plant with pea-sized, shiny berries of what bright colour?

7 A native of Guatemala, the colourful *Odontoglossum grande* is one of the easiest orchids to grow in a living room. What is its common name?

8 *Rhipsalidopsis* or Easter Cactus and *Schlumbergera* or Christmas Cactus are similar in appearance. Apart from their flowers, how can they be distinguished?

[handwritten: FLAT] *[handwritten: ROUNDED]*

9 The ferns *Davallia canariensis* and *Platycerium bifurcatum* (pictured below) each have a common name drawn from the animal world. What are they?

10 Of the following plants, which is the odd one out in that it is a climber usually grown as a trailing pot plant?
(a) *Ficus elastica* (b) *Ficus pumila* (c) *Ficus benjamina*

11 What is the original or alternative name applied to the *[handwritten: Kentia]* palms we now usually call the genus *Howeia*?

12 The small perennial genus *Achimenes* thrives on treatment that would be detrimental to most other plants – treatment that has earned it what common name?

1 What is the name of this 18th-century Palladian house in Norfolk (shown above), whose grounds were designed by the landscape artist Humphry Repton?

2 Adapting the principles of some of the machinery used in the cloth factory of which he was foreman, what tool did Edwin Budding patent that proved to be a boon to the majority of gardeners?

3 Which Moorish garden was begun in the 11th century, completed in 1369 and, along with the Generalife, is one of the few outstanding examples still surviving in Granada?

4 According to the Victorian code of flowers, which messages did the following flowers convey?
(i) Lilac (ii) Rose (iii) Red tulip
(a) I love you (b) First love (c) Love

5 Started in 1844 and completed four years later, the magnificent curved-glass Palm House at Kew was created by which of the following?
(a) Decimus Burton (b) Isambard Kingdom Brunel
(c) Christopher Wren

6 For which particular genus of plants has the writer and plant breeder Tony Clements won numerous awards?

7 The walls constructed around great country houses to exclude animals were sometimes built in an ornate fashion often referred to as serpentine. By what other term was this design known?

8 John Tradescant designed the original terrace, Queen Elizabeth I lived there as a girl, and the gardens feature a lime walk, a maze, two parterres and a knot garden. Which Hertfordshire house is being described?

9 In 1938 a roof garden in Kensington, still in existence today and called at the time 'The Hanging Gardens of London', was first opened to the public. On the roof of which famous store was it situated?

10 What name is given to this plant container (pictured right) developed by Dr Nathaniel Ward in 1833 to facilitate the transportation of living plant specimens?

11 Which French Impressionist painter originally created the recently restored flower and water gardens at Giverny, southwest of Paris?

12 The National Rose Society was founded in 1876 by Dean Hole, who was inspired by a visit to a Nottinghamshire miners' flower show. Where are the society's present-day headquarters?
(a) Kew (b) Wisley (c) St Albans

ROUND
TWO

With its beautifully coloured, fringed flowers borne on short stems, the deciduous, winter-flowering *Pleione formosana* is an ideal plant to grow indoors on a shady windowsill, and in some mild areas it will survive outside in a sheltered rock garden. Which appear first, the leaves or the flowers?

1 The half-hardy *Argyranthemum frutescens* is more generally known as White Marguerite, but what colour is the bushy, tender perennial *Felicia amelloides*, which is sometimes also called a marguerite?

2 Is *Clematis recta* (shown above) a herbaceous species, best planted in the border, or a climber?

3 What name do gardeners give to a young plant soon after seed germination when it has just a single, unbranched stem?

4 The Autumn Crocus does not in fact belong to the *Crocus* genus, from which it differs in that its corm is oval in shape and not flat or round. What is the botanical name of the Autumn Crocus?

5 The rock garden plant *Lewisia cotyledon* (pictured right), which produces white-veined, pink flowers in May or June, sheds its rosette of leaves around October or November. True or false?

6 The Snake's Head Fritillary or *Fritillaria meleagris*, one of around 85 species in the genus, has a wide range of plain, spotted or chequered flower colours, and makes an ideal plant for the wild garden. Does it grow best in dry or moist conditions?

7 The common names of many plants have biblical connotations, an example being the early summer-flowering, lanceolate-leaved *Polemonium caeruleum*. By which of the following is it popularly known?
(a) Aaron's Rod (b) Jacob's Ladder (c) Solomon's Seal

8 Wallflower, Forget-me-not, London Pride and Phlox are all native European plants. True or false?

9 *Iberis*, which originates in southern Europe and Great Britain, is ideal for town gardens as it is tolerant of smoke and grime. What is its common name?

10 The marginal plant *Peltiphyllum* or Umbrella Plant is grown mainly for its unusual foliage. To which of the following is it related?
(a) Saxifrage (b) Primula (c) Broom

11 *Mesembryanthemums* (shown right) are suitable plants for banks, rock gardens and border edges, but what weather condition is needed for the daisy-like flowers to open?

12 Grown mainly for its magnificent mid-green or bronze, serrated-edged leaves, by what name is the *Ricinus* more frequently known?

1 *Lagerstroemia indica* (pictured right) will survive only in the milder areas of Britain. The genus is named after the Swedish patron of science Magnus Lagerstroem, but what is the species' common name?

2 *Enkianthus* species are deciduous or semi-evergreen shrubs and trees with attractive autumn colour. They produce their small bell-shaped flowers in late summer. True or false?

3 *Gleditsia triacanthos* is a deciduous spreading tree with a thorny trunk and glossy, fern-like, light green leaves which turn yellow in autumn. By which of the following names is it also known?
(a) Honey Locust (b) Caspian Locust (c) Hornet Tree

4 As its common name suggests, *Arbutus unedo* or Strawberry Tree produces orange-red, strawberry-like fruits (shown left) as well as having attractive bark. When does it flower?

5 *Parthenocissus quinquefolia*, a self-clinging, deciduous climber originating mainly from China and the Himalayas, is known to most gardeners by which name?

6 Some sub-shrubs produce a horizontal spreading or arching stem which grows above ground and roots at its tip, forming a new plant. What are such stems known as?

7 According to legend, when Christ's betrayer hanged himself from its branch, *Cercis siliquastrum* (pictured right) blushed with shame. What is its common name?

8 What colour are the mature berries borne by the shrubs *Berberis wilsoniae* and *Gaultheria procumbens*?

9 'Grey Owl', 'Blue Star' and 'Skyrocket' are all widely grown varieties of conifers, but to which of the following genera do they all belong?
(a) Junipers (b) Pines (c) Yews

10 What is the common name of *Aloysia triphylla* (shown above), which is often dried for use in potpourris?

11 The hardy, evergreen, flowering shrub *Pieris* thrives in lime-rich soil. True or false?

12 What colour are the flowers produced by the shrubs *Eucryphia*, *Chionanthus* and *Carpenteria*?

1 The popular and widely cultivated herb Sage (pictured right) belongs to a genus of around 700 species of annuals, perennials and mainly evergreen sub-shrubs, many of which are used as summer bedding or mixed border plants. Can you name this genus?

2 A crumbly soil that is easily worked and raked to a tilth is best described as feathery. True or false?

3 Vegetables belonging to the family Cruciferae are among those most susceptible to attack by Flea Beetles. Name two root vegetables at risk.

4 Which greenhouse fruit has a male form called 'Atlas', a female form called 'Hayward', and another form known as 'Jenny', which is said to bear both male and female flowers?

5 What plant is more usually grown for its head of leaves, which is used as a salad vegetable, but also has attractive sky blue flowers (shown left), making it ideal for growing in a mixed border?

6 The Cardoon, grown for its young leaves and stalks, is related to which other vegetable?
(a) Celery (b) Globe Artichoke (c) Chicory

7 What colour are the currant varieties known as 'Baldwin', 'Wellington XXX' and 'Westwick Choice'?

8 The hardy annual Corn Salad (pictured right) is cultivated for its leaves, which are used when young and crisp in winter and spring salads. By what other name is it often known?

9 Which fruit is affected by the virus disease yellow edge, the symptoms of which are most obvious around September?

10 'Bedford Fillbasket' 'Winter Harvest', 'Early Half Tall' and 'Greyhound' are all commonly grown varieties of vegetables. Three of them are Brussels Sprouts; which is the odd one out in that it is a form of cabbage?

11 Grown outdoors primarily for ornamentation, *Punica granatum* (shown left) will, under the correct greenhouse conditions, produce yellow, orange or red fruit with a leathery rind enclosing pulpy red flesh and numerous seeds. By what name is it more usually known?

12 In order to crop Curly-leafed Kale by Christmas, in which month should the first seeds be sown?

1 Name this shrub (pictured above), which can be grown as a conservatory plant and produces densely packed flowers in a variety of colours that darken as they age, resulting in a bloom of two or more colours.

2 In which part of the world is the natural habitat of the air plant *Tillandsia usneoides*, which is also called Spanish Moss?

3 The trailing stems and green, silver and purple leaves of *Ceropegia* make it an ideal plant for a hanging pot or basket and also give rise to some of its common names. Which of the following is not one of them?
(a) Rosary Vine (b) Hearts Entangled (c) King of Hearts

4 The popular *Aspidistra* is easily recognized by its spear-shaped, ribbed, dark green leaves. Where on the plant might you occasionally see its mauve and brown flowers?

5 *Aechmea*, *Tillandsia*, *Billbergia* and *Vriesea* all belong to which exotic group of plants that also includes the edible pineapple?
(a) Cacti (b) Bromeliads (c) Orchids

6 The large-flowered house or conservatory plant *Epiphyllum* is sometimes known as the Orchid Cactus, but is it in fact an orchid, a cactus or neither?

7 The dark green, heart-shaped leaves and clusters of red and white flowers of *Clerodendrum thomsoniae* make it a spectacular plant for growing up a cane frame or in a hanging-basket. Sometimes called Glory Bower, by what other common name is it known?

8 The popular conservatory pot plant *Browallia* is much prized for its long-lived, vivid flowers, in which of the following colours?
(a) Red (b) Yellow (c) Blue

9 *Impatiens*, which is easy to grow in a bright room that is well ventilated on warmer days, is known to almost everyone as Busy Lizzie. Which of the following is not an alternative common name?
(a) Patience Plant (b) Wait-and-see (c) Patient Lucy

10 Which one of the following genera in the cactus family includes the species popularly known as Bunny Ears, Cinnamon Cactus and Cottonpole Cactus?
(a) *Parodia* (b) *Opuntia* (c) *Rebutia*

11 What is the popular name of this plant (shown right), which is closely related to the Monkey Puzzle, reaches heights of over nine metres (30 feet) in the wild, and originates in an island in the Pacific?

12 Match the bulbs listed below with the flowering seasons:
(i) Hyacinth (ii) Lily
(iii) Snowdrop
(a) Winter (b) Spring
(c) Summer

6 What is the name of the gardens on the Wirral, now the University of Liverpool's Botanic Gardens, from which the nursery owner and seedsman A. K. Bulley dispatched George Forrest in search of the remarkable collection of oriental plants currently housed there?

7 Fern frond, Windsor-style, scrolled, and Gothic are all examples of garden benches or seats that have stood the test of time. Can you name the popular bench design that is named after a famous neo-classical English architect?

8 One of the teams on BBC radio's *The Gardening Quiz* is led by *Round Britain Quiz* regular Irene Thomas. Which actor from a long-running radio series captains the other?

1 The original 24 hectares (60 acres) of land on which these gardens (pictured above) were based were given to the Royal Horticultural Society in 1903 by Sir Thomas Hanbury. They are now three times this size and attract many thousands of visitors each year. Where are they?

9 The gardens of which house, originally started in 1842 by James and Maria Bateman, were recently re-established by the National Trust?

2 Ancestral home of the Earls of Bradford, Weston Park boasts a 300-year-old, 21 metre (70 foot) Oriental Plane tree among its copious attractions. In which county is Weston Park?
(a) Warwickshire (b) Gloucestershire (c) Shropshire

10 Name the 17th-century herbalist (shown right) whose book *The English Physician* was for more than a century the authoritative work in its field, and which has had an indirect but powerful influence on the status of herbalism as a modern-day alternative therapy?

3 More and more gardeners are now using coir as an environmentally friendly replacement for peat. What is the natural source from which coir is derived?

4 The chief interest of a dendrologist is trees, but what plants are guaranteed to excite a pteridologist?
(a) Ferns (b) Grasses (c) Fungi

11 Seen in the gardens of many country houses, of what are ball and cylinder, capped mushroom and cakestand all traditional designs?

5 The 1992 British Garden Festival was held in Wales, but at which of these towns was it sited?
(a) Ebbw Vale (b) Cardiff (c) Swansea

12 Name the chairman of *Gardener's Question Time*, who spends his off-duty time tending his half-hectare (one acre) garden in Chepstow?

ROUND THREE

The yellow, daisy-like *Doronicum* provides a dense bank of colour in a bold, mixed planting such as this one, and also makes a good container plant. It flowers throughout the spring and if, regularly dead-headed, will bloom again the following autumn. By what name is this plant commonly known?

7 The *Astrantia* is a hardy herbaceous perennial often grown in mixed borders in this country, but from which continent does it originate?
(a) Europe (b) Australia (c) America

1 At which time of the year does *Bergenia cordifolia* (shown above) or Elephant's Ear produce the first of its attractive bell-shaped flowers?
(a) Spring (b) Early summer (c) Mid-summer

8 What is the common name of this fragrant flower (shown right) whose blooms open so rapidly that its petals move visibly?

2 *Alstroemeria* or Peruvian Lily grows from an underground bulb. True or false?

9 Snowdrop is a winter-flowering, bulbous plant which is best divided and replanted while still 'in the green'. True or false?

3 Which of the following common names is given to a species of the *Amaranthus* genus of half-hardy annuals?
(a) Love-in-a-mist (b) Love Apple (c) Love-lies-bleeding

10 The bushy Night-scented Stock or *Matthiola bicornis* belongs to the genus *Matthiola*, but of which genus is the border plant Virginian Stock the most common species?

4 What word describes the angle between a leaf and a stem from which further growths or flower buds arise?

5 Which of the following situations would best suit the *Matteuccia* (pictured left) or Ostrich Feather Fern?
(a) Partly shaded and moist
(b) Sunny and arid
(c) Deeply shaded and dry

11 This genus comprises 30 species of hardy herbaceous perennials (pictured left). It is closely related to the *Anemones*, under which name its members were formerly known and are still sometimes listed, *vulgaris* being a European species. Can you name this genus?

12 What name is given to a mutation caused by a change, accidental or induced, in the genetic make-up of a plant, giving rise to a shoot with different characteristics to those of the parent plant?

6 When transplanting seedlings what name is applied to the peg or stick used for making holes in the soil?

1 The genus *Lavatera* (pictured right), whose members have trumpet-shaped, hibiscus-like flowers, contains a species that is normally sold as *L. olbia*. From which region of the world does this species originate?
(a) South Pacific (b) Indian Ocean (c) Mediterranean

2 What common name is given to the fleshy, brightly coloured fruit of the rose?

3 Which of the following is the common name of the deciduous bushy shrub *Cotinus coggygria*?
(a) Calico Bush (b) Burning Bush (c) Smoke Bush

4 The early summer-flowering shrub *Menziesia* will thrive on a lime-rich soil. True or false?

5 The bright red berries of the Mountain Ash (pictured left) were once used as bait by bird-catchers, from which practice it gets the alternative common name of Fowler's Service-tree. To what genus does it belong?

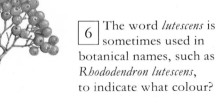

6 The word *lutescens* is sometimes used in botanical names, such as *Rhododendron lutescens*, to indicate what colour?

7 *Fuchsia*, *Calluna* and *Kerria* are all shrubs that are suitable for growing in a small garden, but which of these is the only evergreen?

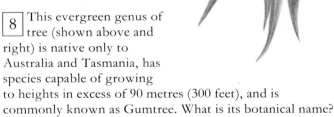

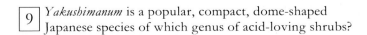

8 This evergreen genus of tree (shown above and right) is native only to Australia and Tasmania, has species capable of growing to heights in excess of 90 metres (300 feet), and is commonly known as Gumtree. What is its botanical name?

9 *Yakushimanum* is a popular, compact, dome-shaped Japanese species of which genus of acid-loving shrubs?

10 The tree *Populus tremula* is known as the Trembling Poplar because its leaves tremble in the slightest breeze. By what other common name is it often known?

11 The hard, white wood of *Euonymus europaeus* was once used to make an essential item for the wool industry, from which the tree received what common name?

12 *Buxus*, *Pyracantha* and *Forsythia* are all attractive shrubs for hedging, but which one is not evergreen?

1 To which genus do the grapefruit (pictured right), thought to be native to southeast China, lemon and lime all belong?

2 Which vegetable of the *Brassica* genus has dwarf-growing varieties called 'Cambridge Special' and 'Dwarf Green'?

3 *Heterodera rostochiensis* is probably the most serious pest to potatoes, checking growth and causing seriously infected plants to die. What is its common name?

4 What is the common name of *Ocimum basilicum* (shown below), the leaves of which may be used fresh or dried as a flavouring for soups, meats and fish?

5 'Boskoop Giant' is black, 'Red Lake' is red and 'White Versailles' is white. What are they?

6 In the list below, which is the odd one out and why? (a) 'Reliance' (b) 'Tender and True' (c) 'Marshall's Showmaster'

7 Can you name the household object that is produced from the dried and bleached interior of the fruit from a member of the cucumber family?

8 Which plant is often cultivated in this unusual terracotta container (pictured right) to prevent the delicate fruit crop coming into contact with the soil?

9 Short-rooted varieties are best for an early or forced crop, intermediate-rooted are larger and slower growing, and long-rooted are grown as a late-maturing crop. What vegetable is being described?

10 What is the name of the poison contained in the leaves of the rhubarb plant *Rheum rhaponticum*?

11 Which vegetable, of which 'Camus de Bretagne' is a popular variety, is more usually grown from offsets, or rooted suckers, than seeds?

12 Can you name the vegetable often cultivated as a quick-growing catch crop, of which 'Rowell' and 'White Vienna' are among the most popular varieties?

1 *Medinilla magnifica* (pictured left) requires consistent warmth, some shade and reasonably high humidity to flourish. Given these conditions it will produce its colourful bracts in a wide variety of hues. True or false?

2 The species *Oncidium ornithorrhynchum* or Dancing Doll Orchid produces arching spikes covered with a mass of flowers that appear in late spring or early summer. True or false?

3 *Vallota* is a bulbous plant with long, narrow, green leaves and scarlet, funnel-shaped flowers. What is its common name, which includes the name of an English town?

4 During its active growth period the Aluminium Plant or *Pilea cadierei* (pictured right) should be watered to which of the following degrees?
(a) Sparingly (b) Moderately
(c) Plentifully

5 What name is given to the group of plants, such as *Crassula*, *Echeveria* and *Kalanchoe*, that have thick, fleshy leaves or stems adapted to life under arid conditions?

6 Of the two indoor plants Yellow Jasmine and White Jasmine, which is a climber and which a rambling shrub?

7 By what name is the common houseplant *Monstera* more frequently known?

8 Name the brilliantly flowered, leaf-shedding climber that grows to a height of 1.5–2.5 metres (5–8 feet), requires a minimum night temperature of 8°C (45°F) and has hybrids called 'Poulton's Special' and 'Mrs Butt'.

9 *Azalea*, *Cyclamen* and *Poinsettia* will grow better and last longer in a cool room rather than one which is too warm. True or false?

10 What is the country of origin of the *Beloperone* or Shrimp Plant, which has brownish, overlapping bracts?

11 The hybrid cross between the Madagascan and Canary Broom is an elegant, arching plant (shown above) that is ideal for the conservatory. What is its common name?

12 What is the common name of the popular foliage plant *Maranta*, probably derived from its unusual habit of folding its leaves at night?

1 Where does this fanciful display of shapes and figures (pictured above) form part of what is probably the finest example of 18th-century topiary?

2 'Capability' Brown's lake and John Vanbrugh's bridge are located in which famous Oxfordshire estate?

3 Robert Fortune was the first of the Victorian plant hunters into China, from where, disguised as a native, he was able to smuggle enough plants into India and Ceylon to establish which now thriving industry?

4 During the reign of which monarch did the Botanic Gardens at Kew achieve their 'royal' status?

5 Which of the following names is given to a commemorative feature (shown right), often seen in parkland around a country house and usually sited at the end of an avenue or on a prominent rise?
(a) Column (b) Obelisk
(c) Tower

6 What term describes the style of garden architecture pioneered in the 19th century by Sir Charles Barry, incorporating stone terraces linked by steps and decorated with balustrades, sculpture and vases, and which may be seen at Harewood House and Holkham Hall?

7 Which Norfolk-based breeder is the driving force behind the rebirth in popularity of the old rose and is the author of *Classic Roses* and *Twentieth-Century Roses*?

8 The *Yellow Book* contains details of private gardens in England and Wales that are open to the public. By which of the following organizations is it published?
(a) The National Trust (b) The National Gardens Scheme
(c) The Royal Horticultural Society

9 Who is this famous gardener (pictured right), poet, novelist and former gardening correspondent of the *Observer*, and which distinguished diplomat did she marry in 1913?

10 Though it is widely known as an amusement park, which Staffordshire country house has magnificent gardens created by the Earl of Shrewsbury which include a conservatory by Abraham as well as a spectacular collection of magnolias, rhododendrons and rare trees?

11 Can you name the garden in Wales that commands views of Snowdonia, is famed for its collection of rhododendrons and contains a former pin mill?

12 Which famous landscape gardener and artist presented 'before and after' paintings to his clients in his, now much sought after, *Red Books*?

ROUND
FOUR

One of the most popular plants for the home,
where it is generally grown for its boldly
patterned, nettle-like foliage, the *Coleus* also
makes a suitable bedding plant. When grown in
this way, should it be treated as an annual, to
be discarded after the first season, or grown on
from year to year?

7 *Nerine* is a genus of bulbous, autumn-flowering plants with many hybrids. Can you name the hardiest species (pictured right) in the genus?

8 What name is given to the fine, crumbly surface of the soil?

9 *Hyacinthoides non-scripta* is called the Bluebell in England. By what name is it known in Scotland?

1 The *Zantedeschia* (shown above) is grown for its beautiful, funnel-shaped spathes. In which part of the world did it originate?
(a) South America (b) South Africa (c) South Australia

10 The common name of which popular garden flower may be prefixed by the words African, Cape, French, Marsh and Pot?

2 Charm, pompom and spray are all non-disbudded types of which popular garden flower?

3 What is the meaning of the Latin word *elegans*, as in the name *Zinnia elegans*?

11 Which one of the two plants *Rheum palmatum* and *Rheum rhaponticum* is not edible?

4 What name is given to the form of vegetative propagation whereby a plant is lifted during dormancy, separated into two or more portions and replanted?

5 The stems of bright red or orange, papery calyces produced by the species *Physalis alkekengi* are commonly used for winter flower arrangements. What is this plant's common name?

6 What word describes the bulb-like, underground storage organ consisting mainly of a swollen stem base usually covered with a papery skin, as in the genus *Crocus*?

12 The delightful *Aquilegia vulgaris* (pictured above) has a number of common names, but which of the following does not apply?
(a) Columbine (b) Summer Snowdrop (c) Granny's Bonnet

1 During June and July this attractive variegated form of *Cornus controversa* (shown left) will produce broad, flat clusters of what colour flowers?

2 The leaves of the *Robinia* genus of trees and shrubs are often described as pinnate. What does this tell us about their formation?

3 Which one of the following plants requires an acid soil in order to thrive?
(a) *Ceanothus* (b) *Kalmia*
(c) *Sambucus*

4 What is the generic name of this free-seeding shrub (shown right), which originated in China and is now often grown to attract butterflies?

5 What type of form or habit is indicated by the Latin word *fruticosa* when used as part of a plant name, such as *Phlomis fruticosa*?

6 What descriptive common name is given to the trees *Acer rufinerve*, *Acer capillipes* and *Acer pensylvanicum*?

7 Which of the following three plants will never produce ornamental fruit?
(a) *Berberis* (b) *Viburnum* (c) *Euphorbia*

8 Native to many parts of Europe, including Britain, this *Betula* (pictured left) is one of the most widely grown garden trees. One reason for its appeal is the silvery bark, to which it owes its common name of Silver Birch. Another of its attractions, namely the graceful, semi-weeping habit of growth, is reflected in the tree's species name. What is it?

9 What genus of at least 500 plant species is best planted in a well-drained, sandy loam in a sheltered, semi-shaded position and has a genus name which is a combination of the Greek words for rose and tree?

10 What distinctive leaf colouring is common to the White Poplar, Weeping Silver Lime and Common Whitebeam?

11 What is the most frequently used name given to the tree *Davidia involucrata* (shown right), which was brought to this country by Ernest 'Chinese' Wilson in the 19th century and is sometimes called the Dove Tree or Ghost Tree?

12 What is the largest flowering shrub in the world, covering half a hectare (one acre) of ground in California and producing hundreds of thousands of blooms during the flowering season?

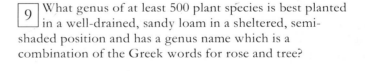

1 The perennial plant *Foeniculum vulgare* (pictured left) is a popular culinary herb, but how is it more likely to be labelled on the supermarket shelf?

2 'Early Rivers', 'Merton Bounty' and 'White Heart' are all popular varieties of which single-seeded fruit?

3 Approach, bridge, crown and saddle are all types of which form of vegetative propagation?

4 The fruit of the Hazel tree or *Corylus avellana* is most commonly known as the hazelnut (shown above). By which other name is it sometimes known?
(a) Macadamia (b) Cobnut (c) Pecan

5 Match the following varieties of Broad Bean with their appropriate type:
(i) 'Express' (ii) 'Bonny Lad' (iii) 'Green and White'
(a) Longpod (b) Windsor (c) Dwarf

6 Most of the varieties of which hardy, spring-flowering fruit trees are related to *Malus sylvestris*, which grows wild in Europe and Asia?

7 Carrots come in a variety of shapes and sizes, but are the popular exhibition carrots 'St Valery' and 'New Red Intermediate' best described as long-rooted or short-rooted?

8 'Arran Pilot', 'Kerr's Pink' and 'Red King' are all varieties of what garden vegetable?

9 The fruit of *Cucurbita maxima* is eaten in America as a vegetable or pie filling, but in Britain it is more often grown for showing. What is it?

10 When the maggots of *Psila rosae* attack the roots of young carrots, celery and parsnips the plants may wilt and eventually die, and older plants are ruined by the tunnels eaten out by them. What is this enemy of the vegetable gardener?

11 The parent of the modern European varieties of pear (pictured right) is native to Europe and western Asia. Can you provide its botanical name?

12 Which of the three varieties of celery listed below is not self-blanching; that is, its stalks need to be artificially blanched by either earthing them up or covering them with paper collars or inverted pots?
(a) 'Giant White' (b) 'Ivory Tower' (c) 'Celebrity'

1 The tropical plant *Canna* (shown right) is grown mainly for its richly coloured spikes of gladiolus-like flowers. What is its common name?

2 *Hedychium* or Ginger Lily, a summer-flowering plant that is grown for its fragrant, orchid-like blooms, is a native of which country?
(a) Chile (b) India (c) Africa

3 What name is given to a modified leaf located at the base of a flower pedicel, which may be conspicuous and highly coloured when it is associated with an inflorescence, as in the *Poinsettia*?

4 *Pellionia* is a genus of tender, evergreen creepers with attractively patterned, multi-coloured leaves. In which of the following ways should they be watered during their active growing period?
(a) Sparingly (b) Moderately (c) Plentifully

5 The moisture-loving plants known as Umbrella Grass and Egyptian Paper Rush are two of over 500 species in which genus?

6 Two of the following plants will survive in a cool greenhouse, but which one requires a temperature in excess of 16°C (61°F) to thrive?
(a) *Phalaenopsis* (b) *Hibiscus* (c) *Fritillaria*

7 *Campanula isophylla* is a trailing plant, ideal for hanging baskets or for setting on a pedestal. How is it more commonly known?

8 Originating in Colombia and related to *Anthurium*, the species *wallisii* (pictured below) and the hybrid × 'Mauna Loa' have bright green, lanceolate leaves and a column-like spike of white flowers arising from a white, ovate spathe. This genus is commonly known as White Sails or Peace Lily, but what is its botanical name?

9 What term is given to the cultivation of plants without soil, using specially prepared solutions of mineral salts?

10 The habit of *Syngonium* or Arrowhead Plant can best be described as bushy. True or false?

11 Which of the three phrases listed below is the correct name for the plant *Cobaea*?
(a) Knife-and-fork Vine
(b) Bottle-and-glass Vine
(c) Cup-and-saucer Vine

12 Of which country is the distinctive *Callistemon* (shown left), commonly known as the Bottlebrush, a native?

27

1 A sprig of a fragrant evergreen shrub, carried at her wedding by Queen Victoria (pictured left) and then planted at Osborne House, has produced progeny used in the wedding bouquets of successive royal brides. Name the shrub.

2 What was the name of the 17th-century Governor General of Canada after whom a genus of plants was named?
(a) Pierre Magnol
(b) Michel Begon
(c) Leonard Fuchs

3 In which of the years listed below was the Royal Horticultural Society flower show first held in the grounds of the Chelsea Royal Hospital?
(a) 1827 (b) 1913 (c) 1947

4 A bowl filled with dried petals from sweet-smelling flowers with a fixative of spices to prolong the fragrance is often used to keep the rooms of houses smelling fresh. What is it called?

5 Built in 1761, the Chinese pagoda is one of the best known of the many attractions at the Royal Botanic Gardens, Kew. Who was responsible for the creation of this impressive structure?

6 *Aubrieta*, the genus of low-growing evergreen perennials, is named in honour of the Frenchman Claude Aubriet. What was his profession?
(a) Botanist (b) Author (c) Flower painter

7 Name the gardener and best-selling author of *The Scented Garden*, whose own gardens at Barnsley House are featured often in British and American magazines?

8 Which of Henry VIII's wives, whose name is commemorated in one of the gardens there, was born at Hever Castle in Kent?

9 Name the preservation and conservation organization, which also owns or runs many impressive gardens, that was founded in 1895 by a lady, a churchman and a knight?

10 On which island off the northeast coast of England can you see a fort converted to a house by Edwin Luytens and a walled garden designed by Gertrude Jekyll?

11 The Tivoli Gardens are probably best known as a place of entertainment but are equally popular for their huge display of flowering plants. In which European city are the Tivoli Gardens to be found?

12 Originally planted in the grounds of their monasteries by the monks, what name is given to this low-growing type of garden (shown below) today?

ROUND FIVE

The grounds of Anglesey Abbey in Cambridgeshire are a blend of formal and free landscaping. They were laid out in the early to middle years of this century mainly to house the collection of statuary, an example of which is seen here, collected by which of these lords?
(a) Fairbairn (b) Fairfax (c) Fairhaven

1 A native of North America, *Eupatorium purpureum* (pictured above) is best grown in a moist position. At which time of the year are its flowers, which are attractive to blue butterflies, produced?

2 What word is used to describe blooms, particularly those of some chrysanthemums, with petals falling outwards and downwards and overlapping like feathers on a bird?

3 Which one of the botanical names listed below refers to the genus of plants popularly known as marigolds?
(a) *Calathea* (b) *Calendula* (c) *Callistemon*

4 Because of the ill effects that are suffered as a result of swallowing its poisonous seed capsule *Datura stramonium* is commonly known in America as Devil's Apple. By what name is this plant generally known in Britain?

5 The herb *Galega* (shown above), a tall bushy plant suitable for the back of a border, acquires its family classification as a result of its pea-like flowers. In which family group is this genus listed?

6 Its large green leaves and tall sprays of white flowers make *Crambe cordifolia* an ideal plant for the back of a border. To which vegetable is it related?

7 Popular with the Elizabethans, *Dictamnus* is said to give off a fragrant aroma of lemons when ignited, a fact which gives rise to its common name. What is it?

8 'Amsterdam', 'Deliverance', 'Moon Mirage' and 'Esta Bonita' are all giant-flowered varieties of which popular plant that produces spikes of funnel-shaped blooms?

9 *Penstemon* is a genus of hardy alpine, and hardy and half-hardy border species that have tubular, open-mouthed flowers and are largely intolerant of wet conditions. They originate in the Americas. True or false?

10 The vernacular name for the *Rudbeckia*, popular for its long-lasting cut flowers, is derived from the shape of the centre of these flowers. What is it?

11 The only species of *Puschkinia* (pictured right) that is in general cultivation in Britain is also known as Striped Squill. To which of the following plants is it related?
(a) *Primula* (b) Lupin (c) *Scilla*

12 The genus *Senecio* contains about 3000 hardy, half-hardy and tender plants, some with grey or silver, often felted leaves. Which term best describes their flowers?
(a) Daisy-like (b) Poppy-like (c) Crocus-like

1 What name is given to a reproductive body containing an embryo often accompanied by food reserves and enclosed within a protective coat?

2 If they are grown in an alkaline soil, blue-flowered varieties of *Hydrangea* will turn pink unless the soil is treated with which chemical compound?

3 The *Eccremocarpus* (shown right), which can survive British winters if grown in a sheltered position, has a common name reflecting its South American origins. What is it?

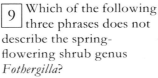

4 Link the following hybrid varieties with the appropriate plants:
(i) 'Nelly Moser'
(ii) 'Elizabeth Harkness'
(iii) 'Blue Peter'
(a) Rose (b) Rhododendron
(c) Clematis

5 The southern European broom *Genista aetnensis*, with its profusion of fragrant, yellow, mid-summer flowers, is most often referred to by which common name?
(a) Sicilian Broom (b) Mediterranean Broom (c) Mount Etna Broom

6 The Atlas Cedar, Deodar and Western Hemlock all belong to which genus of trees?
(a) Yews (b) Pines (c) Cypresses

7 The flowers of two of the three shrubs commonly known as Californian Lilac, Bluebeard and Beauty Bush are blue. Which is the odd one out in that its blooms are pink?

8 The hardy deciduous shrub Wormwood (pictured right) has tall, slender stems of silvery leaves and yellow flowers, and was formerly used in the production of which alcoholic beverage?

9 Which of the following three phrases does not describe the spring-flowering shrub genus *Fothergilla*?
(a) Produces fragrant flowers (b) Prefers acid soil
(c) Is evergreen

10 *Sophora japonica* originates in China, Korea and, as its name suggests, Japan, but from which of the following countries did Sir Joseph Banks introduce *S. microphylla* and *S. tetraptera* in 1771?
(a) Chile (b) New Zealand (c) India

11 The hardy deciduous and evergreen shrub *Ligustrum*, which is much used for hedging, is susceptible to Honey Fungus which may gradually spread along the whole hedge. What it the shrub's common name?

12 This plant (shown left) belongs to a genus containing about 100 species of summer-flowering deciduous trees and shrubs. There are many tender, half-hardy and hardy hybrids in cultivation with habits that range from bushy to trailing. What is the name of this genus?

1 Which herb (pictured left), familiar as a garnish and flavouring for stuffing, soups and sauces, is said to neutralize the odour of garlic if eaten immediately afterwards?

2 The fungal disease *Stereum purpureum* is common on plums, particularly 'Victoria' varieties, and may cause branch die-back or even the death of some trees. How is it more usually known?

3 Which vegetable, usually grown under glass in Britain, has varieties called 'Gipsy', 'Triton' and 'Canape'?

4 Which of the following statements cannot be applied to the raspberry (shown right)?
(a) Grows wild in Iceland
(b) Prefers dry, alkaline soil
(c) Likes sun or some shade

5 The name of which vegetable may be prefixed by the words Egyptian, Welsh or Potato to produce three of its various forms?

6 As their names suggest, 'Atlantic Giant', 'Mammoth' and 'Hundredweight' are all large varieties, but of which garden vegetable?
(a) Cauliflower (b) Pumpkin (c) Marrow

7 Before technology produced rigid wire and steel rods, supports for use in the kitchen garden were obtained by frequently coppicing the twiggy branches produced by which of the following trees?
(a) Willow (b) Hawthorn (c) Hazel

8 What do the loose-leaf lettuce varieties 'Lollo Rosso' and 'Rossalita' have in common with the cos variety known as 'Little Leprechaun'?

9 Used as a basic flavouring for curries and in chutneys and pickles, the seeds of this herb (pictured right) should be stored in airtight containers to improve their flavour. Which herb is it?

10 During which two months of the year is it considered most beneficial to sow swede seeds in order to avoid the risk of mildew?

11 What unusual commercial products are derived from the giant cabbage *Brassica oleracea* 'Longata', a famous tourist attraction in the Channel Islands for more than two centuries?

12 Which of the following conditions is not recommended when growing blackberries?
(a) Well drained, water-retentive soil (b) Sun or partial shade (c) Lime-rich soil

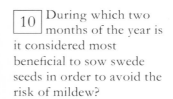

1 The evergreen *Crossandra infundibuliformis* (shown above) is a native of southeast Asia requiring artificial heat to survive British winters. What is the recommended minimum night-time temperature?
(a) 7°C (45°F) (b) 13°C (55°F) (c) 18°C (65°F)

2 The fern *Asplenium bulbiferum* produces young ferns from brown bulbils which appear on the upper surface of the fronds. What common name has it earned as a result?

3 Two of the following plants will survive in an unheated conservatory providing the temperature remains above freezing, but which of the three needs a minimum night temperature of 16°C (61°F)?
(a) *Agapanthus* (b) *Clerodendrum* (c) *Strelitzia*

4 *Tibouchina urvilleana*, with its velvety, prominently veined leaves and striking saucer-shaped flowers of rosy purple to violet, is the only species in its genus that is generally grown as a house plant. Can you supply one of its two common names?

5 The Maidenhair Fern is one of the most popular because it is so easy to grow. What is the genus name?
(a) *Acanthus* (b) *Adiantum* (c) *Abutilon*

6 When grown as a house plant, the *Acorus* has an erect, compact habit, produces large, bright red flowers and requires soil that is permanently saturated. True or false?

7 The *Calceolaria* genus includes species suitable as rock garden or bedding plants, while the tender varieties are widely grown as flowering pot plants. Which of these is not one of its common names?
(a) Pocket Flower (b) Slipper Flower (c) Pouch Flower

8 Among the easiest of succulent plants to cultivate, *Echeveria* species are grown chiefly for their beautiful coloured leaves. Give the common name of the red-flowered *E. setosa*, which reflects its country of origin.

9 Under the right cultural conditions the evergreen shrub *Coffea arabica* or Coffee Plant may, after three or four years, produce fragrant, star-shaped flowers of which colour?

10 Plants in the orchid family always have flowers of six segments. Which of the following is not an orchid?
(a) *Dendrobium* (b) *Gardenia* (c) *Vanda*

11 Because it produces plantlets on its older leaves, this plant (pictured right) has earned the common names Piggy-back Plant, Mother of Thousands and Youth-on-age. What is its botanical name?

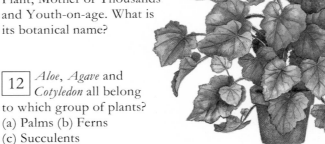

12 *Aloe*, *Agave* and *Cotyledon* all belong to which group of plants?
(a) Palms (b) Ferns
(c) Succulents

1 What was the original use of this building (shown above) in the grounds of Felbrigg Hall in Norfolk?

2 In which Devonshire garden is there a pinetum featuring a magnificent avenue of Monkey Puzzle trees, each planted on a raised platform or mound?
(a) Bicton (b) Castle Drogo (c) Saltram House

3 Which former Carthusian monk, teacher and physician of the 16th century is commemorated in the name of a genus of solanaceous plants?
(a) Anders Sparmann (b) Otto Brunfels (c) Carl Thunberg

4 The internationally renowned flower festival known as Floriade was held in 1992 in which of the following European countries?
(a) Belgium (b) Holland (c) Switzerland

5 Which 19th-century French naturalist and zoologist, commemorated in the name of a species of small deer, introduced a *Clematis* and a *Prunus* species to Europe, both of which bear his name?

6 What is the name of the gardener and writer for *Gardeners' World* magazine who is also a regular on the Radio Essex programme *Down to Earth*?

7 Dorothy Vernon's Walk at Haddon Hall is named after the 16th-century heiress who lived there and eloped with her lover, but for which flowers is this Derbyshire garden best known?

8 Name the alpine specialist who was known affectionately as 'Gussie', was a friend and fellow plant hunter of Reginald Farrer and is commemorated in the name of a species of *Primula* which he discovered.

9 Considered by many to be one of the finest woodland gardens in this country, Leonardslee was laid out by the athlete, big-game hunter and botanist Sir Edmund Loder from 1889 onwards. In which county is Leonardslee?
(a) Surrey (b) Hampshire (c) West Sussex

10 This artist (pictured right) set off at the age of 40 to paint exotic flowers in many countries and, encouraged by Sir Joseph Hooker, gave her collection to Kew Gardens, where it is displayed in a gallery opened in 1882 that bears her name. Who was she?

11 The parasitic plant *Rafflesia* is reputed to produce the largest flower in the world, with blooms sometimes measuring up to 0.9 metres (3 feet) in diameter. To which region is it native?
(a) Malaysia (b) South America (c) New Zealand

12 *Forsythia*, the genus of popular deciduous shrubs, is named after the 18th-century gardener and writer William Forsyth. What was his nationality?
(a) Irish (b) Welsh (c) Scottish

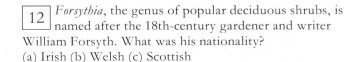

ROUND SIX

The name *Clematis* is derived from the Greek word *klema*, meaning 'vine branch', which is an apt description of this beautiful plant which adorns walls, trellises and pergolas across the land. Can you identify the species climbing up this wrought-iron frame, which includes the varieties 'Abundance' and 'Etoile Violette'?

1 *Hylotelephium* (formerly *Sedum*) *spectabile* (shown left) or Ice-plant, a late summer-flowering succulent and a great attraction for butterflies, originates in which country?
(a) Chile (b) South Africa (c) China

2 What is the main soil characteristic indicated by a reading of less than seven on the pH scale?

3 Which of the plants listed below does not have its origins in South or Central America?
(a) *Verbena* (b) *Zinnia* (c) *Lavatera*

4 Which of the following methods is chiefly used in the propagation of chrysanthemums?
(a) Layering (b) Cuttings (c) Grafting

5 Which of the following common names is given to the spring-flowering perennial *Primula denticulata* (pictured below) with its red or purple flowers?
(a) Cowslip (b) Drumstick Primula (c) Primrose

6 The woolly coating of the leaves and stems of the Great Mullein (shown left) or *Verbascum thapsus* was once used in the production of which household object?
(a) Bootlaces (b) Dishcloths (c) Candlewicks

7 What is the common name that is most often given to the herbaceous plant *Geranium*?

8 When applied to grasses or bamboo, what word is used to describe the stem, which is usually hollow?

9 Name the method employed to break the dormancy of the seeds of some hardy plants whereby they are exposed to a low temperature for a period prior to sowing?

10 'Baby Doll', 'Blue Tit', 'Jade' and 'Cinderella' are all dwarf varieties of which popular garden flower?

11 The cultivated species of Wallflower produce blooms in a variety of hues, but what colour are the flowers borne by the wild form?

12 The *Astilbe*, which has plume-like, red, pink or white, flower heads and fern-like foliage, needs dry soil conditions in order to thrive. True or false?

1 This popular evergreen shrub (pictured right), originating from India, China and Japan, has hybrid varieties called 'Donation', 'J. C. Williams' and 'November Pink'. What is it?

2 What is the name of the fruit of *Crataegus monogyna* or May, which follows the white, heavily scented flowers in autumn?

3 What is the common name of the southern American evergreen shrub *Yucca filamentosa*, as suggested by its stiff, thorn-tipped leaves?

4 What attractive feature is common to the bark of Paper-bark Maple, London Plane and Paper Birch trees?

5 *Malus* (shown left) is widespread as a garden tree grown for its mainly ornamental fruit. What is the common name of this genus?

6 *Dentatus* and *azureus* are species belonging to a genus of shrubs which prefer the shelter of a warm wall to encourage their panicles or umbels of star-shaped, blue flowers. What is this genus?

7 A newly planted hybrid tea rose must be pruned back to the fourth or fifth outwardly facing bud. True or false?

8 What unusual formation is described by the Latin word *contorta* when incorporated into the name of such plants as *Corylus contorta*?

9 What word describes the removal or shortening of stems, branches or roots in order, among other things, to promote the growth of flowers and/or fruits?

10 'Silver Queen', 'Madame Briot' and 'Silver Milkmaid' are all varieties of which evergreen tree?
(a) Pine (b) Holly (c) Yew

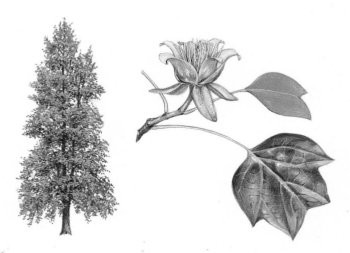

11 The genus *Liriodendron* or Tulip Tree (pictured above) consists of only two species, one of which is from China. Name the continent of origin of the other.

12 The Irish Yew or *Taxus baccata* has an attractive, slow-growing, yellow-leaved form whose foliage changes with age to green with yellow edges. What is the botanical name of this form?

1 Orange trees may be successfully grown in tubs under glass in Britain, including the species (shown right) most commonly used in the production of marmalade. What is its common name?

2 As applied to young fruit trees, what are cordon, dwarf pyramid and fan-trained?

3 'Hokus', 'Crystal Apple' and 'Zeppelin' vary greatly in size, shape and colour but they are all varieties of which popular vegetable?

4 Which of the following three fruit varieties is the odd one out and why?
(a) 'Golden Noble' (b) 'Grenadier' (c) 'Denniston's Superb'

5 This hardy annual, culinary herb (pictured left) produces five-petalled, blue, star-shaped flowers that are attractive to bees and are used to flavour salads and fruit cups. What is its common name?

6 'Fuseau' is one of the two varieties in general cultivation of a hardy perennial grown for its edible tubers, and has white flesh under its purple skin. Which winter vegetable is being described?

7 What half-hardy annual vegetable has varieties called 'Snowball', 'Autumn Giant' and 'English Winter', and will crop from March through to December if planted in deep, rich, consolidated soil?

8 Curly-leaf, plain-leaf, rape, and leaf-and-spear all describe types of which source of spring greens, virtually untroubled by the usual *Brassica* pests?

9 Musk, canteloupe and winter are three classifications of a fruit grown in Britain. Recommended varieties with good flavour include 'Charentais', with orange flesh, 'Ogen', which has green flesh, and 'Sweetheart', with scarlet flesh. What fruit is it?

10 The blackberry (shown below) can be grown in all parts of Britain and fruits in late summer or early autumn on growths produced the previous season. Which of the following is not a variety of blackberry?
(a) 'Himalaya Giant'
(b) 'Oregon Thornless'
(c) 'Lloyd George'

11 Carrots are divided into long-rooted, intermediate-rooted and short-rooted types. Into which of these groups does the exhibition carrot 'St Valery' fall?

12 'Gulliver', 'Pickwick' and 'Red Knight' are all dwarf varieties of Runner Bean producing pods of 15–20 centimetres (6–8 inches). True or false?

1 *Sansevieria trifasciata* (pictured left) is a well-known house plant grown for its stiff, erect, lance-shaped leaves. Which member of the family is it commonly named after?

2 *Amaryllis belladonna* and *Hippeastrum* both belong to the same genus of plants. True or false?

3 What word describes a plant adapted to live above the soil, usually adhering to tree branches or mossy rocks, with orchids and bromeliads providing good examples?

4 *Abutilon* or Flowering Maple, *Miltonia* or Pansy Orchid and *Streptosolen* or Marmalade Bush all originate in which region of the world?

5 What colour are the tubular, waxy, scented flowers of *Stephanotis floribunda*, borne from May to October?

6 There are only two species in the genus *Washingtonia* (shown right). Both are relatively easy to grow indoors and they make attractive feature plants. Which of the following types of plants are they?
(a) Ferns (b) Shrubs
(c) Palms

7 The common name of the small shrub *Brunfelsia pauciflora* reflects the fact that each bloom opens violet purple, fades to blue, becomes almost white and is dead by the fourth day. What is it?

8 *Dixonia* is suitable for growing only in the mildest areas of Britain, but makes a good conservatory plant when young. What is its common name?

9 The meaning of the Latin word *edulis* as in *Passiflora edulis* could be of great practical value in certain circumstances. What does it convey?

10 Which of the following common names is not applied to this plant (pictured above)?
(a) Rose Mallow (b) Rose of Jericho (c) Rose of China

11 Which type of plant is *Parodia aureispina* or Golden Tom Thumb?
(a) Cactus (b) Fern (c) Palm

12 The *Narcissus* produces trumpet-shaped flowers in shades of yellow, white and cream, borne on a long, leafless stem. By what name is this type of stem known?
(a) Spadix (b) Stolon (c) Scape

1 A fine example of this garden feature (shown above) may be seen at Hampton Court Palace. What is it?
(a) Pleached alley (b) Laburnum walk (c) Stilt hedge

2 What French term was given to the long, rectangular strip of turf running between canals or driveways that was a feature of many of the grand gardens of Britain and the Continent?

3 Both Kew Gardens and Alton Towers feature a Chinese pagoda in their grounds, but which of these pagodas is also a fountain spurting a jet of water 21 metres (70 feet) into the air from its top?

4 Can you name the gardener, writer and one-time host of *Gardeners' World*, which often visited his home, 'The Magnolias'?

5 In the grounds of which royal residence will you find an oak tree planted by George VI in 1937, another by Elizabeth II in 1977 and a third reputed to be 850 years old?
(a) Balmoral (b) Sandringham (c) Windsor

6 At which London palace is there a grapevine of the Black Hamburg variety that was planted in 1769 and still bears over 500 bunches of fruit each year?

7 What is the structure, common in grand and modest gardens alike, which is often erected over a pathway and adorned with flowering climbers?

8 Which 18th-century landscape gardener involved in redesigning the gardens at Hampton Court Palace was described by the author Horace Walpole as 'the father of modern gardening'?
(a) 'Capability' Brown (b) Christopher Wren (c) William Kent

9 In addition to sponsoring plant collectors such as George Forrest, A. K. Bulley was the founder and owner of which famous seed company?
(a) Bees (b) Suttons (c) Dobies

10 An enthusiastic gardener, writer, plant hunter and broadcaster, he received the Gold Veitch Memorial Medal from the Royal Horticultural Society, of which he has been a member for around 30 years. Who is he?

11 The Crystal Palace (pictured above) and the Great Conservatory at Chatsworth were both the creation of which famous 19th-century head gardener?

12 Great Dixter, which has gardens designed by Edwin Luytens with planting advice from Gertrude Jekyll, is to be found in which of these English counties?
(a) Kent (b) East Sussex (c) Hampshire

ROUND SEVEN

Long prized in their native Asia, tulips were introduced to Europe in the mid 16th century, and achieved instant popularity. They are classified in a number of different divisions, one of which, Darwin, is seen here. Name two of the other groups, one named after a famous artist and another after a tropical bird.

1 The bulb *Galtonia candicans* (shown left) is suitable for planting in borders or pots and is closely related to the hyacinths. In which season does it flower?

2 Many of the species of *Silene* are weeds but some are suitable as rock garden plants. Sometimes referred to as Catchfly, what is their most frequently used common name?

3 Pinks and carnations have been popular since classical times for their beautiful flowers and, in many cases, their fragrance. Under what botanical heading are they classified?

4 What name is given to the removal of the growing point of a stem in order to promote a branching habit or to induce the formation of flower buds?

5 One species of *Myosotis* or Forget-me-not is the floral emblem of the US State of Alaska, but to which part of the world is *M. sylvatica* indigenous?
(a) North America (b) Great Britain (c) China

6 *Salvia viridis* (pictured right) is unusual in that the stem bears both flowers and bracts. It was once used to make what commercial commodity?

7 *Ligularia dentata*, sometimes wrongly included in the genus *Senecio*, was introduced to this country by Ernest Wilson in 1900. Does it favour dry or moist soil?

8 Commonly known as Bugle, this ground-cover plant bears whorls of blue, tubular, lipped flowers on erect stems, and has a purple-leaved form called 'Atropurpurea'. What is its botanical name?

9 The plant Wake Robin (shown above) belongs to a genus distinguished by having all their parts, including leaves, sepals and petals, in groups of three. How, as a result, is the genus known botanically?

10 Native to Asia, *Eremurus* or Foxtail Lily bears spikes of flowers that may reach a height of 3 metres (10 feet). Do they grow from a bulb or a fleshy root?

11 'City of Haarlem' 'Delft Blue' and 'Pink Pearl' are all widely cultivated varieties of which popular, spring-flowering, bulbous plant?
(a) Dutch Hyacinth (b) Grape Hyacinth (c) Tulip

12 *Pyrethrum*, which has bright green, feathery foliage and daisy-like flowers, is now classified botanically within which other genus of plants?

1 What term describes the loosely twining habit of plants, for example some *Clematis* (pictured above), which often climb by pushing their stems up through other plants?

2 Shrubs of the deciduous and evergreen genus *Viburnum* flower variously in spring, summer or winter, either on the bare branch or with the leaves. When does the evergreen *V. tinus* produce its flowers?

3 What can be described as an often pendulous spike or narrow raceme of unisexual flowers covered in scale-like bracts and usually falling as a whole?

4 The berries of *Ruscus aculeatus* (shown left) are produced only if plants of both sexes are grown together. Its leaves too are unusual in that they are in fact flattened stems. What are such stems called?

5 *Eucryphia*, which needs a sheltered, semi-shaded situation to flourish, does best with its roots in a cool, moist position and its crown in the sun. True or false?

6 The evergreen shrub *Garrya elliptica* bears grey-green catkins from mid winter to early spring, from which it derives its common name. Which of the following is it?
(a) Lamb's Tail Bush (b) Silk Tassel Bush
(c) Goldilocks Bush

7 The rampant and vigorous climber *Polygonum baldschuanicum* produces panicles of pink or white flowers in summer. What is its common name, which reflects both its origin and habit?

8 In order to thrive and produce its delicately coloured, fragrant flowers, the tender shrub *Melia azedarach* or Persian Lilac requires a hot, dry situation. True or false?

9 Beech trees produce hairy fruits which ripen in the autumn to release edible nuts. Is the shape of these nuts best described as round, triangular or square?

10 The slow-growing shrub *Osmanthus ilicifolius* (pictured left), along with other forms commonly known as False Holly and Sweet Olive, bears tubular, scented flowers during September and October. Is it evergreen or deciduous?

11 Approximately how many years does it take the American conifer *Picea breweriana* or Brewer's Spruce to produce its female cones?
(a) 5 years (b) 15 years (c) 30 years

12 Although banned at one time because of its association with the Celtic winter solstice festival, what plant is now used throughout Britain for its decorative berries?

43

1 The soft but tough-skinned larvae of the Cranefly or Daddy-long-legs are common garden pests that feed chiefly on the roots of plants. By what name are they commonly known?

2 At the Ministry of Agriculture's experimental horticultural station in Kent, sandwiched between 'Malden Wonder' and 'Milton' are probably the only examples of 'Maltster' surviving today. What are they?

3 *Eriobotrya japonica* (shown above) is a common sight in the warmer regions of southern Europe, where its fruits may be bought from markets and shops in late winter and spring. What is the plant's more usual name?

4 Of the three listed varieties, which is a rhubarb, which an apple and which a gooseberry?
(a) 'Sunset' (b) 'Whitesmith' (c) 'Hawke's Champagne'

5 The potato variety 'Pink Fir Apple' is, of course, pink, 'Golden Wonder' is russet, but what colour is the main crop variety 'Maris Piper'?

6 At the end of the 19th century a fruit, of which 'Jenny Lind', 'Weasel' and 'London' were contemporary varieties, was celebrated in its own anthem, telling of the challenge for supremacy thrown down by two popular varieties. What type of fruit was it?

7 The herb *Prunella* (pictured right) is common in many countries, spreading rapidly by means of its probing rhizomes and abundant seed. By what name is this medicinal plant generally known?

8 Which popular fruit is grouped, according to shape, into the classes bergamot, rounded, conical, waisted and calebasse?

9 Though it is moderately easy to grow, the broccoli variety 'Purple Sprouting' will not be ready to cut until approximately 9 to 11 months have elapsed after sowing. True or false?

10 Which vegetable, a half-hardy annual grass that crops throughout August and September, has F_1 hybrids known as 'Aztec', 'North Star' and 'First of All'?

11 What varieties of vegetable are 'Green Bush', 'Long Green Striped' and 'Tiger Cross'?

12 What was the function of the terracotta bells (shown left) that were used in Victorian gardens and had removable lids to allow the crop to be inspected?

1 Young specimens of *Sparmannia africana* (pictured left) make handsome house plants, producing striking white flowers with purple-tipped stamens. By which of the following names is it commonly known?
(a) African Orchid
(b) African Lily
(c) African Hemp

2 What is the correct name for the milky sap, sometimes poisonous, produced by such plants as *Euphorbia* and *Ficus*?

3 Although not a member of the *Lilium* genus, the *Haemanthus*, which originates on the African continent, has acquired a name which suggests otherwise. What is it?

4 *Stromanthe* species, close relatives of *Maranta* and *Calathea* species, require high humidity allied to normal room temperatures, making them ideally suited to the terrarium or bottle garden. True or false?

5 *Aechmeas* (shown right) belong to the bromeliad family of plants, which in their natural state are mainly epiphytic or tree-living plants that collect rainwater in the central 'cup' formed by their leaf rosettes. When cultivated indoors in a container should they be grown in lime-rich or lime-free soil?

6 The succulents commonly known as Chandelier Plant and Devil's Backbone were species originally placed within the genus *Bryophyllum*. Under which genus heading are they now listed?

7 Link the following plants with the appropriate descriptive terms:
(i) Croton (ii) *Sempervivum* (iii) *Muscari*
(a) Succulent (b) Bulb (c) Foliage plant

8 The slender and graceful house plant *Cocos nucifera* or Coconut Palm (pictured right) is one of how many species in the genus *Cocos*?

9 *Chlorophytum*, one of the most common and popular house plants, is often known as Ribbon Plant or Spider Plant. In order to thrive it should be kept in a dimly lit situation. True or false?

10 Japanese Sedge, the most widely cultivated form of the ornamental grass *Carex*, has feathery, widely arching stems, making it an ideal foil for bolder plants. From what underground storage organ do the stems arise?

11 *Rebutia* is a cactus, *Phoenix* is a palm, but to which botanical grouping does *Oncidium* belong?

12 The Poor Man's Orchid is often grown in frost-free conservatories but is also suitable for annual borders and for cutting. Which of the following is its botanical name?
(a) *Schisandra* (b) *Schizanthus* (c) *Schefflera*

7 Which British romantic poet was forced to sell his ancestral home, Newstead Abbey, for financial reasons in 1817, with a monument to his beloved Newfoundland dog Bosun still in evidence in the grounds near the Eagle Pond?

8 *Clematis montana* and *Anemone vitifolia* were among the plants cultivated from seed and sent to this country by a botanist and wife of a Governor-General of India, who is also remembered in the name of an ornamental pheasant. Who was she?

1 This house (shown above) was built in the 17th century but altered in the middle of the next by Robert Adam. The gardens, however, were mainly created from 1925 by Major Edward Compton and are considered among the finest in North Yorkshire. Can you name this place?

2 Which 19th-century gardener, writer and rose expert introduced and edited the influential magazine *Floral World* in 1858?

3 French onion sellers, with their berets, bicycles and strings of onions, were once a familiar sight in Britain's cities. From where in France did they bring their produce? (a) Brittany (b) Normandy (c) Provence

4 The Englishmen C. H. Curtis and W. Gibson, and the Frenchman Guillaume Beaumont, were all recognized as authorities on which garden art?

5 Persian jar, inscribed vase and pastryware are all types of what container?

6 Name the television and radio broadcaster, presenter of *Gardeners' Direct Line* and his own *World of Flowers*, and author of *A Passion for Plants*, who gardens in the heart of the Yorkshire Dales.

9 Plant boxes were made in many different styles, including this one (pictured right), which had one side hinged so the tree could be removed for root pruning. Can you name it?

10 What is the name of the unusual garden in County Down that is rich in topiary and tender plants, such as the Banksian Rose, and features the cement figures of the Ark Club on the Dodo Terrace.

11 Which garden structure became popular because, according to a contemporary admirer, "... a fragment could be more eloquent and thought-provoking than a complete artifact" and "grandeur in decay could have a special beauty"?

12 Now grown in gardens the length and breadth of Britain, the vegetable *Solanum tuberosum* was first introduced to this country by which of the following celebrated travellers? (a) Charles Darwin (b) Captain Cook (c) Sir Walter Raleigh

ROUND EIGHT

Henry Hoare set about creating the magnificent gardens at Stourhead in 1744. The classical building shown here, which lies across the lake, contains statues of gods and heroes, and is a miniature version of a surviving 2nd-century Roman temple, after which it is named. Can you say what this building is called?

1 The colourful petunia (shown above) will produce its spectacular flowers from late spring to early autumn provided it is planted in a shady position. True or false?

2 The words 'Flore Pleno' in a plant's botanical name, as in *Ranunculus ficaria* 'Flore Pleno', suggest what about the appearance of its blooms?

3 Which type of food storage system does the dahlia have? (a) Corm (b) Tuber (c) Bulb

4 As suggested by both its botanical and common names, a species of the genus *Nicotiana* is used in the production of something in everyday use around the world. What?

5 The popular cottage garden plant *Althaea* produces single or double, funnel-shaped flowers, in a wide range of colours, on stems that may reach 2 metres (6 feet) in height. What is it popularly called?

6 The deciduous alpine *Leontopodium alpinum* (pictured left), which has small, white, groundsel-like flowers, is much better known to gardeners (as well as lovers of musicals) by what common name?

7 A small individual flower that forms part of a large head or cluster is known by which of the following terms? (a) Floret (b) Raceme (c) Carpel

8 The Water Lily is a common garden pond plant with a tuber-like rhizome. How often should this be divided to ensure healthy growth?

9 What term is used to describe the depth to which soil is dug with a fork or spade, usually around 25–30 centimetres (10–12 inches)?

10 Which of the following plants does not produce aromatic foliage? (a) *Salvia* (b) *Primula* (c) *Geranium*

11 Young leaves from Bergamot (shown above) may be used in salads, tisanes and potpourris. Sometimes known as Sweet Bergamot or Bee Balm, what is this plant's generic name?

12 Which word, when preceded by Trumpet, Spring, Marsh or Willow, will produce the common names of four species of popular hardy perennial?

1 What common name is given to the evergreen coniferous tree *Picea abies* (pictured left), widely used throughout Europe as a Christmas tree?

2 Most of the species belonging to the genus *Pittosporum* are native to which part of the world?
(a) South America (b) Asia
(c) Australasia

3 Name the technique of maintaining a tree in a bushy state by cutting back hard to the main trunk and pruning every one or two years.

4 *Sasa veitchii* is sometimes described as being 'a nuisance' or 'of little garden value', but to which of the following groups of plants does it belong?
(a) Fern (b) Cacti (c) Bamboo

5 The foliage of the Stag's-horn Sumach (shown right) takes on shades of orange-red, purple and yellow from September onwards. To which of the following genera does it belong?
(a) *Robinia* (b) *Rhus*
(c) *Rhamnus*

6 What is the common name of the flat-topped species of cedar originating in Syria and southeast Turkey that grows to a height of 12 metres (40 feet), is frequently found in parks and the gardens of old houses, and of which 'Sargentii' is a slow-growing variety?

7 Its mound-forming habit, aromatic woolly leaves and button-like, yellow flowers make the Cotton Lavender a suitable plant to grow in the front of a border or as a low hedge. What is its generic name?

8 The bright yellow flowers of the tree *Koelreuteria* (pictured left) give rise to its more frequently used name Which of the following is it?
(a) Golden Show
(b) Golden Chain
(c) Golden Rain Tree

9 What attractive leaf feature is common to *Acer pseudoplatanus* 'Worleei', *Hedera helix* 'Buttercup' and *Taxus baccata* 'Elegantissima'?

10 Which of the shrubs in the following list is not suitable for growing in a rock garden?
(a) *Cotoneaster*
(b) *Fremontodendron*
(c) *Hypericum*

11 As used in such plant names as *Picea glauca*, what is indicated by the term *glauca*?

12 *Styrax japonica* (shown right) derives its common name of Japanese Snowbell from its pendent, white, fragrant flowers. Is it deciduous or evergreen?

1 Native to the Middle East and cultivated in many temperate and sub-tropical areas of the world, figs (pictured left) may be successfully grown outdoors as bush trees in warmer, sheltered areas of Britain. In the north they are best fan-trained against south-facing walls. Which of the following varieties is most often grown in Britain?
(a) 'Brown Beauty'
(b) 'Brown Turkey'
(c) 'Brown Prince'

2 Which popular native European fruit includes the varieties 'Packham's Triumph', 'Doyenné du Comice' and 'Louise Bonne of Jersey'?

3 Which smooth-skinned sport or mutant of the peach has a variety known as 'Lord Napier', more often grown under glass in Britain?

4 There are two types of fennel. One, *Foeniculum vulgare*, is a culinary herb. The other, which is a sub-species of this plant, is a vegetable. What is its botanical name?

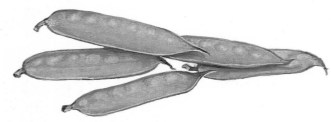

5 What name is more commonly used for the type of peas (shown above) that are sometimes referred to as Snow Peas or Sugar Peas?

6 What name is given to the white, crisp and slightly bitter hearts of the salad vegetable *Cichorium intybus*?

7 Which vegetable, available in a variety of colours, is produced by the F_1 hybrids 'Corvet', 'Green Duke' and 'Express Corona'?

8 The tender green leaves of this perennial herb have a mild onion flavour and are often added to egg, cheese and fish dishes. What is its common name?

9 What is the correct name for the vegetable that is more popular in Europe than in Britain, is sometimes called Turnip-rooted Celery, and is susceptible to slugs, Carrot Fly and Celery Fly?

10 Part of this plant (pictured right) has a pungent, peppery flavour and is traditionally grated and mixed with cream to make a condiment or flavouring for sauces. What part is used?

11 The stock of strawberry plants is most commonly increased by which form of natural propagation?

12 'Sandwich Island' is a variety of which little-known vegetable grown for its long, pale yellow roots with a fleshy texture and the flavour of oysters?

1 To which widespread family of plants, containing almost 20,000 species, does the South American *Cattleya* belong?

2 The trumpet-shaped flowers of the *Schlumbergera* (pictured right) provide a spectacular, display of colour in the spring. What is its common name, which indicates part of the flowering period?

3 *Sinningia speciosa*, which is also known as Gloxinia and Cinderella Slippers, has bold, bell-shaped flowers and broad, heart-shaped, velvety leaves, making it an ideal feature plant for table-top display. The new growth produced each year arises from a tuber. True or false?

4 *Impatiens* or Busy Lizzie is a popular indoor plant, but what is the meaning of the Latin word *impatiens*?

5 Which one of the following plants is grown for its foliage?
(a) Shrimp Plant
(b) Angel's Tears
(c) Prayer Plant

6 What is the genus of this conservatory climber (pictured left), which is often seen on Mediterranean holidays?

7 Many bromeliads, such as *Guzmania* and *Neoreglia*, have an arrangement of leaves radiating from a crown or distinct centre in an overlapping spiral. What is the technical term for this leaf formation?

8 The Glory Lily differs from the Tiger Lily and the Easter Lily in two distinct ways, one being its tuberous root formation. What is the more obvious difference?

9 Which one of the following plants is a palm, not a fern?
(a) *Pteris* (b) *Adiantum* (c) *Howeia*

10 *Tillandsia* species, which are members of the bromeliad group, differ from other epiphytic or tree-living plants in not having a central cup for collecting rainwater; instead their leaves absorb moisture from the humid air and nutrient salts from its dust content. Under what collective name are such plants sold in garden centres?

11 Native to Natal in South Africa, the Kafir Lily (shown right) has thick stems topped with funnel-shaped, orange flowers among strap-shaped leaves. What is its generic name?

12 Approximately how long does it take for a newly planted *Agave* to produce a flower spike?
(a) 5 years (b) 20 years (c) 50 years

ROUND EIGHT · GARDENS AND GARDENERS

1 The Botanic Gardens on the Isle of Wight (pictured right), which date only from 1970 and include a museum devoted to smuggling, are fast becoming known for their interesting collection of exotic plants. In which resort are the gardens?

2 The flowers, shrubs and trees collected by David Douglas are considered by some to have had more effect on our gardens than the discoveries of any other plant hunter. In the name of which coniferous tree is his work immortalized?

3 Which famous English poet was responsible for landscaping the nearly 2-hectare (4.5-acre) garden at Rydal Mount, Ambleside, where he spent the last years before his death in 1850?

4 Covering 40 hectares (100 acres) and managed by the Forestry Commission, Bedgebury in Kent is home to one of the largest and most varied collections of conifers in Europe. What name is given to such a collection?

5 What name is given to a small bunch of colourful flowers that may or may not be fragrant and is surrounded with a paper frill, greenery or silver foil?
(a) Posy (b) Bouquet (c) Buttonhole

6 Laid out in the 18th century by 'Capability' Brown, the grounds of Syon House are now partly given over to which permanent display of British horticulture?

7 The Royal Botanic Gardens at Kew evolved from the private gardens of two 18th-century female royals; one was created by Princess Augusta, wife of Frederick, the Prince of Wales. Who was responsible for the other?
(a) Queen Anne (b) Queen Charlotte (c) Queen Caroline

8 The Chelsea Physic Garden was founded in 1721 by an Irish physician and one-time president of the Royal Society, whose library formed the nucleus of the British Museum. Can you name him?

9 The gardens at Sissinghurst in Kent are the ones most readily associated with Vita Sackville-West, but at which house near Sevenoaks, Kent, did she create her first garden, between 1915 and 1930?

10 Originating in Central America, the genus *Dahlia* takes its name from the 18th-century botanist Anders Dahl. What nationality was he?
(a) Swedish (b) Danish (c) German

11 The sub-tropical trees, statuary and fountains make the island garden of Isola Bella in Italy one of the great horticultural sights in Europe. On which lake is Isola Bella?
(a) Como (b) Maggiore (c) Lucerne

12 What is the name of the Swedish botanist (shown right) who evolved the system of classification whereby each plant has two scientific names, the first the genus name and the second the species?

ROUND NINE

Asplenium scolopendrium 'Crispum' is a sterile fern and may only be increased by division. As a group, ferns bear neither flowers nor seeds but produce instead tiny capsules on the underside of the fronds. These capsules contain powdery, single-celled bodies capable of reproduction. What are they called?

7 The spectacular *Helianthus* or Sunflower is indigenous to North America, but which of the following states is nicknamed the Sunflower State?
(a) Florida (b) Texas (c) Kansas

8 What is the name of the process in which the coat of a seed is scarred by abrasion in order to speed up water intake and hence germination?

9 'Green Woodpecker', 'Albert Schweitzer', 'Blue Conqueror' and 'Dr Fleming' are all large-flowered hybrids in which genus of bulbous flowering plants?

1 *Pelargonium* (pictured above), the genus of deciduous and evergreen, mainly tender sub-shrubs, contains approximately 300 species. True or false?

2 What word describes a plant derived from crossing any two varieties, sub-species or, occasionally, genera?
(a) Sport (b) Mutant (c) Hybrid

3 A regular feature in many religious works of art and admired for its tall, white, fragrant flowers, *Lilium candidum* is better known as what?

4 In which month do the first blooms appear on garden varieties of *Phlox* such as 'Brigadier' and 'Harlequin'?

5 What is the common name of the popular bedding plant *Dianthus barbatus* (shown right)?

6 Name the portion of old wood that is retained at the base of a half-ripe cutting.

10 *Aruncus* or Goat's Beard (pictured above) is a hardy herbaceous perennial. True or false?

11 At which point on the pH scale is soil deemed to be neutral, i.e. neither acid nor alkaline?

12 The storage organ of the Bearded Iris is a creeping stem with leafy shoots. Is this a tuber or a rhizome?

1 The evergreen plant *Trachelospermum jasminoides* (shown right), sometimes called the Star Jasmine, produces its fragrant flowers during July and August. Which of the following terms best describes its habit?
(a) Bushy (b) Ground cover (c) Climbing

2 The unusual shrub *Halimium lasianthum*, which bears rich, butter-yellow flowers each with a characteristic brown blotch at the base, is native to which country?
(a) Portugal (b) Chile (c) Japan

3 Which of the following terms best describes the habit and form of the conifers Shore Juniper, Flaky Juniper and Temple Juniper?
(a) Prostrate (b) Conical (c) Columnar

4 What is the botanical name of this deciduous tree (pictured left), the genus of which orginated in China and comprises only one species, whose leaves are similar in shape to those of the Maidenhair Fern?

5 What common name is given to the fruit of *Quercus* species, consisting of a thick-walled nut in a scaly, cup-like base?

6 What characteristic is implied by the use of the words *odora* or *odorata* in a plant's nomenclature?

7 The genus of hardy, deciduous, long-lived tree *Ulmus* has species commonly described as Cornish, Jersey and Scots. What is its popular name?

8 The words Chilean, Zig-zag, Arrow and Timber are all prefixes in the common names of which of the following types of plant?
(a) Bamboo (c) Grass (c) Sedge

9 *Paulownia tomentosa* or Foxglove Tree bears spectacular, foxglove-like flowers in erect panicles (shown left). Do these appear before or after the foliage emerges?

10 What word refers to a shoot which arises from below ground level, usually from the rootstock of a plant, such as in the *Syringa* or Lilac?

11 What is the name of this evergreen shrub (pictured right), which prefers the protection of a warm, sheltered wall to encourage it to produce its large, perfumed blooms throughout the summer?

12 Willows form a genus of about 500 hardy, deciduous trees and shubs which vary greatly in size and all bear catkins. What is the name of this genus?

1 Popular as an additive to stews, bouquets garnis, soups and spaghetti dishes, *Origanum vulgare* (shown left) has rose to purple tubular flowers. Give its common name.

2 On which common vegetable garden hand tool would you find a tine?

3 Which of the following tomatoes is particularly recommended for growing in a greenhouse?
(a) 'Tornado' (b) 'Roma'
(c) 'Big Boy'

4 Which unwelcome visitors to the vegetable garden come in varieties known as Strawberry, Common and Banded?

5 Varieties of *Prunus domestica* (pictured right), which produce a crop of fleshy fruit in late summer, are usually budded or grafted onto a rootstock of proven performance, such as 'Pixy'. True or false?

6 The caterpillars of *Hoplocampa testudinae* tunnel below the skin of small fruit and later burrow in their centres, leaving the fallen fruit in June and remaining in the soil until spring. By what common name is this pest known?

7 The heaviest cauliflower grown in Britain (in 1966) was of the variety 'Metropole'. How much did it weigh?
(a) 16.95 kilograms (37 pounds 6 ounces) (b) 20 kilograms (44 pounds) (c) 23.9 kilograms (52 pounds 12 ounces)

8 Which vegetable grown for its edible leaves, which are also attractive enough to justify its planting in the flower border, contains the variety 'Fordhook Giant'?

9 Blackcurrants (shown left), whitecurrants and redcurrants are widely grown for their juicy acid fruits produced in summer. They will thrive in all parts of the British Isles. True or false?

10 What are the distinctly differing culinary uses for *Petroselinum crispum* (Parsley) and *P.c. tuberosum* (Hamburg Parsley)?

11 Which of the fruit varieties listed below is the odd one out and why?
(a) 'Red Gauntlet' (b) 'Talisman' (c) 'Whinham's Industry'

12 Although it may appear to have been done purely for ornament, the training and pruning of young fruit trees also has a practical purpose in that the size and quality of the fruit are improved and it is also more accessible for picking. Can you name the growth form into which this apple tree (pictured right) has been shaped?

1 The daisy-like flowers of *Gerbera* (shown right) appear in a wide range of colours and make excellent cut flowers, while their leaf shape is often referred to as lanceolate. What is meant by this term?

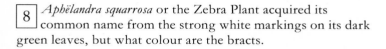

2 *Dracaena draco*, an ornamental foliage plant, is one of the longest-lived species – a specimen in the Canaries is said to be over 1000 years old. What is the plant's common name?

3 What is the minimum night temperature required by the African Violet or *Saintpaulia* in order to survive?
(a) 7°C (45°F) (b) 10°C (50°F) (c) 13°C (55°F)

4 Like all members of its genus, *Cordyline terminalis* or Goodluck Plant (pictured left) requires an atmosphere high in humidity in order to flourish. True or false?

5 Which of the following plants is not suitable for growing in a bottle garden?
(a) *Maranta*
(b) *Saintpaulia*
(c) *Canna*

6 *Streptocarpus* is a small plant with hairy, strap-shaped leaves and stems of foxglove-like flowers. What is its common name, suggestive of its country of origin?

7 The *Poinsettia* is a popular house plant for Christmas decoration, but in its native Mexico it may grow to a height of 3 metres (10 feet). True or false?

8 *Aphëlandra squarrosa* or the Zebra Plant acquired its common name from the strong white markings on its dark green leaves, but what colour are the bracts.

9 *Asparagus plumosus* is grown in the kitchen garden for its edible spears. True or false?

10 The vicious spines and tiny scarlet flowers, like drops of blood, have earned *Euphorbia milii splendens* (shown right) the common name of Crown of Thorns. What other, less well known, 'biblical' name is used for this semi-succulent conservatory shrub?
(a) Christ Plant (b) Moses Plant (c) Bethlehem Plant

11 The common name of the evergreen climber *Cissus* owes much to the plant's Australian origins. What is it?

12 Despite its name and appearance the graceful yet compact Sago Palm (pictured left) is not a palm at all. It belongs to one of the most ancient and primitive families of plants and is thought to have been the food plant of the dinosaurs. What is the name of this family?

1 During a 30-year partnership with the 19th-century architect Edwin Luytens, this artist, gardener, and craftswoman (shown left) was involved in the design of around 300 gardens. Who was she?

2 Which garden feature was first conceived in the 16th century, is constructed from thin wooden laths and is popular in today's gardens where it is used to support climbing plants or to create archways, bowers and see-through dividers?

3 The first full-grown flowering specimen of the Great Water Lily, *Victoria regia*, was produced in Joseph Paxton's vast lily house at which Derbyshire estate?

4 Which of the following names is given to the geometrical arrangement of hedge walls, inter-linked paths, junctions and blind alleys planted in the grounds of many large country houses?
(a) Maze (b) Boskett (c) Labyrinth

5 Which renowned plant collector, son of an equally famous plantsman, commemorated in the botanical name of Spiderwort, introduced the Tulip Tree, Plane Tree and Red Maple to this country?

6 The genus *Buddleia* is named after the Essex man Adam Buddle who, in 1708, wrote an unpublished *English Flora*. What was his occupation?
(a) Doctor (b) Parson (c) Teacher

7 Name the organization established in 1959 which is represented by the initials NAFAS?

8 The gardens at Hidcote Manor were much admired by Vita Sackville-West and include a bathing pool garden, theatre lawn and Dutch style topiary. What is the approximate size of the gardens?
(a) 4 hectares (10 acres) (b) 9 hectares (22 acres)
(c) 26 hectares (40 acres)

9 The largest and most varied collection of rhododendrons in Britain was created by Lionel de Rothschild in the gardens of his country home, Exbury. In which English county is Exbury?

10 Which of the following terms describes a broad roadway or drive lined on both sides with trees, often limes, elms or horse chestnuts, planted at regular intervals?
(a) Alley (b) Arbour (c) Avenue

11 The first great greenhouse erected at Kew (shown above) was built in 1761. What is it called?

12 The herbaceous border, first popularized at the turn of the century, is the essence of many English gardens, but can you name the Jacobean-style house in Cheshire whose famous twin borders were among the first of their kind to be planted in this way in Britain?

ROUND TEN

Although 'Capability' Brown was one of many
designers who made his mark on the gardens at
Chatsworth, he left intact the cascade created in
the French style by Grillet. Which architect built
the Cascade House at its head in 1703?
(a) Thomas Telford (b) Thomas Archer
(c) Robert Adam

1 The *Platycodon* (pictured above) is suitable for a border or a large rock garden. What is its common name, which is derived from the inflated shape of its flower buds.
(a) Balloon Flower (b) Blue Orb (c) Pumpkin Plant

2 The species of *Anthemis* commonly known as Camomile is often used to create small lawns because of its mat-forming habit and the apple fragrance given off when it is trodden underfoot. Which vigorous, non-flowering variety is particularly used for this purpose?
(a) 'Trelawny' (b) 'Truro' (c) 'Treneague'

3 The annual *Helichrysum bracteatum* is grown for its chaffy, daisy-like flowers which stay on the plant throughout its flowering season, giving rise to its common name of Everlasting Flower. In which of the following countries does it originate?
(a) Mexico (b) South Africa (c) Australia

4 What term is given to the removal of faded flowers to prevent seeding or to tidy the appearance of a plant?

5 *Eranthis hyemalis* or the Winter Aconite (shown right) has deeply cut, pale green leaves and will flower from February onwards. What colour flowers does it produce?

6 The hardy perennial *Diascia*, which has glossy, green leaves and shell-like, pink blooms borne from May to July, should be cut back after flowering to encourage subsequent flushes. True or false?

7 Which invasive garden weed, known botanically as *Taraxacum*, takes its common name from the French term meaning 'lion's tooth'?

8 One of the species of *Ornithogalum* is widely grown in Africa for cut flowers which are exported to Britain and last for weeks in water. Name this usually white or cream flower?

9 What is the common name of the herb *Centranthus ruber* (pictured right), which was much used in the Middle Ages but is now more often seen in the herbaceous border?

10 What plant has sprays of blue Forget-me-not-like flowers reflecting its relationship to *Myosotis*, but has approximately 9-centimetre (4-inch), matt green leaves that are rough and heart-shaped?

11 Identify the odd one out in the following list in that it is an Auricula rather than a variety of Sweet Pea.
(a) 'Vera Lynn' (b) 'Terry Wogan' (c) 'George Harrison'

12 Which 'space-age' word features in the common names of *Eruca vesicaria sativa*, which has edible leaves, and *Hesperis matronalis*, which has evening fragrance?

1 Introduced from North America in 1726, *Catalpa* (shown left and below) is often grown for its large, bright green leaves, but it also produces flowers and long, thin seed pods from which it gets what common name?

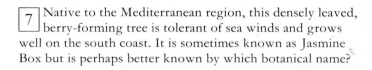

2 What word is applied to an undeveloped branch, leaf or flower enclosed within protective scales?

3 The evergreen trees and shrubs of the genus *Azara* are grown for their foliage and flowers composed of a mass of stamens. What colour are these flowers?

4 *Crinodendron* needs the protection of a sheltered position in the garden or a wall to produce the urn-shaped flowers which give it the common name of Lantern Tree. Does it need acid or alkaline soil?

5 Once known as a magical antidote to the forces of evil and witchcraft, *Ruta graveolens* (pictured right) is now mainly planted for its ornamental, silvery foliage. What is its common name?

6 The common name of *Parrotia persica*, which is grown for its autumn foliage and red clusters of petal-less flowers, reflects its region of origin. What is it?

7 Native to the Mediterranean region, this densely leaved, berry-forming tree is tolerant of sea winds and grows well on the south coast. It is sometimes known as Jasmine Box but is perhaps better known by which botanical name?

8 Which one word when preceded by Greater or Lesser will give the common name of each of the two European species of sub-shrub *Vinca major* and *Vinca minor*?

9 What is the more frequently used name for the *Sambucus* genus of hardy, deciduous shrubs or small trees producing star-shaped, white flowers followed by black, red or blue, shiny fruits?

10 The deciduous, silver-leafed tree *Pyrus salicifolia* 'Pendula' bears clusters of white flowers followed by fruit. Are these 'pears' edible?

11 The native Spanish grass *Stipa gigantea* (shown right) has long flower stems similar to those of Pampas Grass. By what descriptive common name is it generally known?

12 The evergreen genus *Gaultheria*, named after the 18th-century botanist Dr Gaultier, includes the creeping species *G. procumbens*, which produces globose berries in the autumn. What colour are these berries?
(a) Red (b) Yellow (b) White

1 Native to eastern Asia, *Citrus limon*, the Lemon tree (pictured right), is cultivated commercially throughout the Mediterranean region and in many sub-tropical countries. In Britain the tree needs the protection of a heated greenhouse for the production of mature fruits. How long do the fruits usually take to ripen?
(a) 6 months (b) 8 months (c) 12 months

2 Used in Britain at least since the Iron Age, this essential gardening tool has been produced in a number of different designs, including Dutch, Belgian, American round-point, London-treaded and perforated. What is being described?

3 If the variety 'Gladiator' was sown in March, which vegetable crop could be harvested as a result around November?

4 The evergreen shrub sometimes known as Dew of the Sea (shown left) is used to flavour lamb, pork and chicken. Give its more usual common name.

5 Common Fennel is used for flavouring, but which part of Florence Fennel or Finocchio is eaten as a vegetable?

6 What name is given to the disorder affecting cauliflower and broccoli that is caused by a deficiency of molybdenum and results in distortion and a reduction of the leaf blade to the mid-rib?

7 Vegetable Spaghetti, Crookneck and Yellow Patty Pan are all types of which relatively uncommon vegetable?

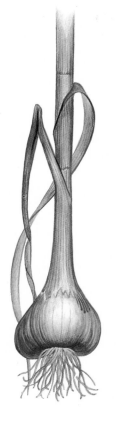

8 What is the name most often given to the bulblets of the Garlic plant (pictured left) used to flavour salads, soups, fish and meat dishes?

9 If mildew-resistant lettuces such as 'Avondefiance' are sown in early August, and covered with cloches with closed ends in September, when should the crop be ready for cutting?

10 Which little-grown perennial vegetable, of which 'Giant Russian' is an outstanding variety, is cultivated for its edible, long, tapering, dark purple to brown roots?

11 What term describes plants, particularly fruit trees, that do not need a pollinator to set fruits and seeds?

12 Having sown Celeriac under glass in March and planted out the seedlings in late May, in which month could you expect to begin lifting the crop?

1 The conservatory plant *Eucomis bicolor* (shown left) bears a spike of star-shaped flowers topped by a bushy tuft of leafy bracts. The spike's resemblance to a tropical fruit has earned the plant what common name?

2 The *Cymbidium* produces flowers in a wide variety of colours and each bloom will last around six weeks. At what time of year are they in evidence?

3 What name is given to the practice of setting a plant container up to the rim in soil, peat, sand etc., to prevent drying out and to protect the root system against fluctuating temperatures?

4 The name of which genus of tender perennials, generally divided into tuberous, rhizomatous and fibrous-rooted types, may be preceded by Eyelash, Beefsteak and King to produce common names for three of its numerous species?

5 Sometimes known as Lipstick Plant or Basket Vine, *Aeschynanthus speciosus* will produce long, tube-like, bright flowers of what colour?

6 *Erythrina crista-galli* (pictured left) may survive outside in sheltered areas but is more usually grown as a conservatory plant for its spikes of brilliant red flowers. To which country is this species indigenous?

7 *Schlumbergera truncata* is a free-flowering succulent often grown as a pot or hanging-basket plant in greenhouses or conservatories. Which of the following is not one of its common names?
(a) Crab Cactus (b) Claw Cactus (c) Goldfinger Cactus

8 *Philodendron bipinnatifidum* is one species in a large genus of plants grown for their magnificent leaves, which uncurl a glistening pale green and darken and thicken with age. Does it originate in South Africa or South America?

9 Given bright, filtered light and a temperature of around 20°C (70°F) the bromeliad *Guzmania* will produce its handsome, brilliantly coloured flower bracts in June or July. True or false?

10 *Anthurium*, *Dieffenbachia* and *Monstera* all belong to the same family of non-woody, tropical plants, Araceae. Which of these is also a member of the family?
(a) *Zantedeschia* (b) *Guzmania* (c) *Hibiscus*

11 Baby's Tears, Freckle Face and Polka-dot Plant (shown left) are all common names applied to one shrub-like foliage house plant needing a minimum temperature of 10°C (50°F). To which of the following genera does it belong?
(a) *Hippeastrum*
(b) *Hippophae*
(c) *Hypoestes*

12 Which word when preceded by Pincushion, Powder Puff, Old Lady or Silver Cluster will complete the common names of various species of the conservatory or house plant *Mammillaria*?

1 Which beautiful Yorkshire gardens, created by John Aislabie in the 18th century, feature the Moon Pools (pictured above) and have magnificent views of the romantic ruin of Fountains Abbey?

2 Created by the Duchess of Montrose and bequeathed to the National Trust for Scotland in 1958, the gardens at Brodick Castle are on which of these islands?
(a) Islay (b) Arran (c) Mull

3 It is generally accepted that the first conservatories to house oranges and other exotic plants were constructed in the 17th century, but by approximately which year did they take on the social role of an additional room for informality and relaxation?
(a) 1800 (b) 1850 (c) 1900

4 The grounds of Hildesheim Cathedral in Germany contain the oldest plant of its kind in the world. It was said to have been planted by Charlemagne, but is probably around 400 years old. What sort of plant is it?

5 Which world-famous nursery, originally based at Turnford in Hertfordshire and specializing in indoor plants, is reputed to have introduced the term 'house plant' into general use in 1947?

6 Calke Abbey in Derbyshire, Felbrigg Hall in Norfolk and Westbury Court Gardens all have fine examples of which bygone feature of the grand country house?
(a) Walled kitchen garden (b) Icehouse (c) Mausoleum

7 The first known botanic garden was laid out at Padua, Italy, in 1545. Which is Britain's oldest, founded in 1621?
(a) Kew Gardens (b) Oxford Botanic Gardens (c) Edinburgh Botanic Gardens

8 A dendrologist, horticultural writer and designer, he invented a wrought iron sash bar which made possible such spectacular buildings as the Palm House at Kew and the Crystal Palace. In 1826 he founded *The Gardener's Magazine*. Who was he?

9 In which offshoot of the gardener's craft was Constance Spry a leading influence?
(a) Plant breeding (b) Flower painting (c) Flower arranging

10 Name the plant collection founded by Gerald Loder in Ardingly, West Sussex, which is now an annexe to Kew Gardens.

11 Can you name the Scottish plant hunter (shown right) who, on an expedition to China earlier this century, collected more than 300 new species of rhododendron?

12 Which English botanist, plant collector and author of the books *My Rock Garden* in 1907 and *Alpines and Bog Plants* the following year, also published eight plays, a novel and six travel books?

ROUND ELEVEN

The strikingly beautiful azaleas, seen here bordering a pathway at the Royal Horticultural Society's garden at Wisley, were formerly treated as a separate genus but they are now included under the same heading as another equally impressive group of trees and shrubs. What is its name?

1 Which genus of moisture-loving plants commonly called Monkey Flower (pictured above) has species known as Monkey Musk and Lavender-water Musk?

2 What term is applied to a plant which requires a permanently wet or moist soil and grows particularly well at the edge of a pool?

3 *Convallaria* or Lily of the Valley, which is grown for its sweetly scented, bell-shaped flowers, grows best in partial shade. True or false?

4 The botanical name of the plant *Tradescantia virginiana* (shown left) honours the 17th-century plant collector and gardener John Tradescant. How is this species more usually known?
(a) Dropwort (b) Lungwort
(c) Spiderwort

5 Match the types of inflorescence listed below with the appropriate plants:
(i) Spikes (ii) Racemes (iii) Panicles
(a) *Gypsophila* (b) Lavender (c) Hyacinth

6 What is meant by the use of the word *officinalis* in the Linnaean system, as used in *Stachys officinalis*?

7 Approximately how many species are included in the genus *Gentiana*?
(a) 37 (b) 250 (c) 400

8 There are several methods of increasing plants by vegetative propagation. Can you name three of them?

9 What is the male reproductive organ of a flower called?

10 The common names of *Billbergia nutans* and *Narcissus jonquilla* 'Flore Pleno' both begin with which royal title?

11 The elegantly shaped bulbous plant *Fritillaria imperialis* or Crown Imperial (pictured above) is indigenous to Venezuela and Colombia. True or false?

12 Known to generations of children for its mouth-like flower which opens when the sides are pressed, what is the name of this popular plant (shown left)?

1 'Pulborough Scarlet', 'Brocklebankii' and 'King Edward VII' are all named varieties of this hardy, deciduous shrub. What is its botanical name?

2 The growing of *bonsai* (pictured right) involves planting the tree in a pot of the correct proportions then regularly pinching out the growth and pruning the roots. Where did this practice originate, over 1000 years ago?

3 The large Lanuginosa group of *Clematis* should be pruned when they have finished flowering. True or false?

4 The unusual shrubs *Salvia microphylla*, *Azara dentata* and *Fuchsia magellanica* all occur naturally in Central or South America. True or false?

5 Which word defines an arrangement of leaves or flowers arising from one point, similar to the spokes of a wheel?

6 Sometimes called Furze or Whin, by what other common name are the evergreen, spiny, flowering shrubs (shown above) of the genus *Ulex* known?

7 The first hybrid tea rose was produced in 1867 by the French nurseryman Guillot, but in what year were hybrid teas officially recognized?
(a) 1871 (b) 1888 (c) 1894

8 Which of the following terms more accurately describes the habit of Black-eyed Susan, Morning Glory and Chinese Wisteria?
(a) Ground cover (b) Twining climber (c) Bushy

9 Plants whose seeds have a protective case are called angiosperms. What name is given to plants that have uncovered seeds, such as conifers, in which the seeds are borne between the scales of the female cone (pictured right)?

10 Which shrub, useful as a climber or as ground cover, has a golden-leafed variety known as 'Buttercup'?

11 The fragrant, spidery flowers of *Hamamelis* (shown left) are often cut for the house. What is its common name?

12 *Juglans regia*, which bears drooping green catkins when mature, and whose wood is used for veneer and gun stocks, is not a native of Britain. True or false?

ROUND ELEVEN · THE KITCHEN GARDEN

1 Some plants, such as strawberries (pictured right), produce aerial roots which, on contact with moist soil, root at the tip and form new plants. What are such roots called?

2 Rhubarb or Ruby is the prefix for the red-leaved variety of which vegetable?

3 Can you name the three main groups into which cultivated beans are divided?

4 Which word refers to the woody stem, often hollow or pithy in the centre, of such plants as the raspberry?

5 'Golden Sunrise' and 'Sutton's Golden Queen' are yellow-fruited forms of which popular salad vegetable?

6 This hardy evergreen shrub (shown below) is the creeping form of a plant used for flavouring food and commercially in soaps, antiseptic agents and the liqueur Benedictine? What is it?

7 What name is given to a trained fruit tree that has a vertical trunk and opposite, horizontal branches arranged at about 30–40 centimetre (12–15 inch) intervals?

8 Name the annual salad plant with the varieties 'Windermere', 'Susan', 'White Heart' and 'Imperial'.

9 In which type of vegetative propagation is a shoot of an individual plant artificially united with the rootstock of another to form one plant?

10 Although it is not cultivated, this spectacular fungus (pictured above) may appear in rural gardens and is delicious to eat. What is its common name?

11 Name the practice that involves excluding light from the stems and/or leaves of vegetables such as celery.

12 At which time of the year will the type of strawberry known as ever-bearing or perpetual crop at intervals?
(a) April to July (b) June to October (c) August to December

68

1 Purple Passion Vine, Violet Nettle and Velvet Plant are all common names applied to this house plant (shown left). What is its generic name?

2 The climbing house or conservatory plant *Thunbergia* originates in the Americas. True or false?

3 On some orchids one stem joint may become swollen with storage tissue, in some cases resembling a bulb. What is this called?

4 Which genus of more than 900 species, containing several house plants grown for their evergreen textured leaves with colourful patterns, includes the species with the common name Iron Cross?

5 A bell jar (pictured right) or an inverted jam jar may be used as a cover for certain house plants. For what purpose is this practice followed?

6 With its trumpet-shaped, bright red or purple flowers, and its vigorous, climbing habit of growth, the *Ipomoea* makes an ideal subject for growing up wires or a trellis in the conservatory. What characteristic of the plant gives rise to its common name of Morning Glory?

7 What is unusual about the diet of the plants Huntsman's Cap, Cobra Plant and Sundew?

8 *Vallota* is an excellent plant for a sunny window and is closely related to and a member of the same family as which other genus of bulbous plant, of which 'Apple Blossom' is a popular variety?

9 *Fittonia* (shown right) is an extremely delicate foliage house plant whose paper-thin leaves, veined in silver or white, have earned it the common name of Snakeskin Plant. In addition to much warmth and humidity, which of the following degrees of light does this plant require?
(a) Deep shade
(b) Reasonable light
(c) Full sun

10 The common name of *Pachystachys lutea* is derived from the appearance of its cone-shaped bracts and white tubular flowers. What is it called?

11 *Opuntia microdasys* is a popular, profusely branching species of cactus whose common name should act as a warning to anyone thinking of handling it. What is it?

12 Having planted a bowl with hyacinth bulbs (pictured left) for indoor use, the container should then be excluded from light until the flower buds appear. True or false?

1 Where in Scotland is there a greenhouse similar to, but much larger than, the one at Chatsworth in Derbyshire?

2 The national collection of hydrangeas is held at the Lakeland Horticultural Society near Windermere. Approximately how many species and cultivars are held?
(a) 60 (b) 140 (c) 320

3 Which famous historical figure created the greatest rose garden ever, with the help of the most respected horticulturalists of the day, at the Chateau de Malmaison at the beginning of the 19th century?

4 Although they were created by various designers, the gardens at West Wycombe Park were the inspiration of the baronet and founder of the infamous Hellfire Club who once lived there. What was his name?

5 Visitors to Cliveden in Buckinghamshire, Newstead Abbey in Nottinghamshire and Tatton Park in Cheshire would all be able to see fine examples of a Japanese garden. True or false?

6 Often to be found in the grounds of country houses, the garden house is designed for the comfort of people rather than the needs of plants. Which of the following structures is not a form of garden house?
(a) Gazebo (b) Pavilion (c) Boskett

7 This pioneering plant collector (shown left) and admirer of Charles Darwin became Director of Kew in 1865. Who was he?

8 Which gardens in the north of England were designed by John Vanbrugh, laid out by George London and Henry Wise, and include a mausoleum, a pyramid and the Temple of the Four Winds (pictured above)?

9 Name the naturalist who sailed around the world with Captain Cook, was a long-serving President of the Royal Society and is commemorated in the name of a genus of Australian shrubs.

10 Which of the following English counties is renowned for the growing of tulips?
(a) Norfolk (b) Lincolnshire (c) Suffolk

11 Following earlier work by Downer and Harkness, which grower, by rigorous selection of seed-raised lupins, produced the popular strain which bears his name?

12 The Regal Lily, *Lilium regale*, with white flowers shaded with purple, was introduced to this country from China in 1904 by an intrepid collector who suffered a smashed leg in his attempt to obtain the plant. Who was he?

ROUND TWELVE

The only native European palm, *Chamaerops humilis* (shown here) was introduced to Britain in 1731 and grows in gardens in the southwest of England and along the west coast of Scotland. Its small size, rarely exceeding 2 metres (6 feet), and fan-like fronds provide clues to its common name. What is it?

1 *Clarkia unguiculata* (shown right) produces a bold display of colour from early summer to early autumn and is useful for mixed borders. Under what genus name was this plant formerly listed?

2 Name the process by which tender and half-hardy plants that have been grown under heated glass are gradually acclimatized to outside conditions.

3 The perennial *Cosmos atrosanguineus*, commonly called Chocolate Cosmos because of the chocolate fragrance of its flowers, grows from a rhizome. True or false?

4 Some species of *Ranunculus* are suitable for rock gardens and alpine houses and two are aquatic. What is the common name of members of this genus?

5 *Pulmonaria officinalis* (pictured left) was once recommended as a herbal treatment for complaints of the lungs, possibly because of its spotted, lung-shaped leaves. When does it flower?
(a) Early spring (b) Summer
(c) Autumn

6 The evergreen, mat-forming perennial *Arabis* belongs to the same family as which one of the plants listed below?
(a) *Clivia* (b) Cabbage
(c) *Clematis*

7 *Incarvillea delavayi*, first brought to Europe by the French missionary Père Jean-Marie Delavay, produces its first Foxglove-like flowers in late spring. Do they appear before or after the leaves?

8 An impressive plant for the wild garden, *Dipsacus fullonum* produces large, spiny, seed heads that are attractive to finches and flower arrangers alike. What is this plant's common name?

9 *Anchusa* is a genus of sun-loving, herbaceous plants, some of which are suitable for the alpine house. What colour flowers are produced by this genus?

10 *Physostegia* derives its common name of Obedient Plant from the fact that when individual flowers are pushed to one side they will stay there, but which of these terms best describes the shape of the flowers?
(a) Bell-like
(b) Snapdragon-like
(c) Primrose-like

11 The Foam Flower (shown right) is a member of a genus related to *Heuchera* and of the same family as Saxifrage. By which of the following names is this genus of rock garden or ground-cover plants known?
(a) *Tiarella* (b) *Tigridia*
(c) *Tolmiea*

12 Which of the following terms best describes the leaves of the popular variety of mat-forming, perennial *Stachys* known as 'Silver Carpet'?
(a) Leathery (b) Woolly (c) Bristly

1 *Tamarix* is a genus containing 90 species of evergreen or deciduous trees and shrubs that can make excellent hedging. They are very wind-resistant and thrive in exposed coastal positions, such as on sand-dunes. True or false?

2 *Lupinus arboreus* (pictured left) is the only shrubby species in a genus made up mainly of herbaceous perennials with spires of pea-like flowers. What is indicated in this context by the Latin word *arboreus*?

3 *Olearia*, originating as it does in New Zealand and Tasmania, is suitable only for sheltered areas of Britain. One species is known as Maori Holly, but what name is usually applied to the genus? (a) Daisy Bush (b) Poppy Bush (c) Buttercup Bush

4 What word describes a plant that lives upon another, taking its nourishment from its host and being incapable of an independent existence?

5 Originating in South America, *Araucaria araucana* may eventually reach heights of 21 metres (70 feet) in this country. Sometimes called the Chile Pine, it is far better known by which other enigmatic name?

6 The hardy shrub *Skimmia japonica* 'Veitchii' will only produce its brilliant red berries, which last from autumn through winter, if a form such as 'Rubella' or 'Fragrans' is planted in close proximity. Can you say why?

7 What colour are the flowers of the deciduous species of *Photinia*, also grown for their foliage and fruit?

8 The planting of which tree (pictured right) was encouraged by James I in an unsuccessful attempt to establish a silk industry in Britain?

9 What can be described as a plant that produces permanent woody stems which normally branch from the base instead of having a single stem or trunk?

10 The deciduous shrubs *Enkianthus campanulatus*, *Fothergilla major* and *Hamamelis mollis* all prefer the same soil condition. Should it be acid or alkaline?

11 *Erica*, *Calluna* and *Daboecia* are all types of which ornamental foliage plant? (a) Heather (b) Grass (c) Bamboo

12 *Ceratostigma plumbaginoides* (shown below), a low-growing shrub that flowers near the end of summer, will benefit from a light pruning around which month? (a) July (b) March (c) November

1. The tree *Laurus nobilis* (pictured left) is often grown as a standard and its leaves are used in cooking with fish, lamb and soups and in bouquets garnis. What is its common name?

2. What term describes the practice of digging into the soil a crop of vigorous, leafy plants sown especially for that purpose?

3. Petit pois are simply immature peas that are gathered from small pods of any garden pea variety. True or false?

4. What could be described as a fleshy, several-seeded fruit without a stony layer around the seeds, which are embedded in pulp as in the gooseberry or tomato?

5. 'Pancho' is an early variety, 'Argenta' a mid-season and 'Catalina' a late variety of which widely grown vegetable?

6. Pennyroyal, Pudding Grass and Lurk-in-the-grass are all names applied to a creeping form of which widely grown, multi-purpose garden herb (shown above)?

7. According to the 1993 *Guinness Book of Records* the longest carrot was grown by Mr Bernard Lavery. Approximately how long was the record breaker? (a) 2.1 metres (7 feet) (b) 3.2 metres (10 feet 5 inches) (c) 4.9 metres (16 feet)

8. With the availability of cheaper ironwork, glass bell jars were replaced with these iron-framed plant protectors (pictured left), which were produced in a number of ornate designs. What collective name was used for these 'miniature greenhouses'?

9. Which vegetable includes the early variety 'Tokyo Cross', which is sown outdoors in April or May, and the maincrop 'Golden Ball', sown in July or August?

10. If grown in a greenhouse in Britain, the plant *Musa acuminata* requires a minimum winter temperature of 10°C (50°F) in order to produce its edible fruit. By what name is this fruit generally known?

11. 'Clemson Spineless' is a popular variety of the greenhouse vegetable okra. By what other name is okra commonly known?

12. The oblong, dull, claret-coloured fruits of this plant (shown right) are produced on shoots of the previous season's growth in July and August. What plant is it?

1 The *Stapelia* (pictured right) derives its common name of Carrion Flower from the unpleasant odour with which it attracts blowflies as pollinators. What purpose is served by the long, delicate hairs that cover its seeds?

2 The orchid-like flowers of *Bauhinia variegata*, often seen in warm holiday locations, give rise to this plant's most widely used common name. What is it?
(a) Japanese Orchid Bush (b) Orchid Tree (c) False Orchid

3 Often the result of poor air circulation, powdery and downy are two types of which disease affecting the leaves of some indoor plants?

4 A native of West Africa, this member of the *Ficus* genus (shown left) is grown as a house or conservatory plant for its large, glossy, slightly crinkled leaves. What is its common name?
(a) Mistletoe Fig (b) Fiddle-leaf Fig (c) Cascading Fig

5 The attractive house plant *Grevillea robusta*, commonly known as Silky Oak, has handsome, fern-like foliage, and flowers very rarely appear. In which country does it originate?

6 The genera *Yucca* and *Agave* belong to the same botanical family. True or false?

7 *Cuphea ignea* is suitable as a summer-flowering pot plant and derives its common name from its tubular, orange-red flowers with a dark band and white ring at the mouth. Which of the following is it?
(a) Torch Flower (b) Cigar Flower (c) Firefly Flower

8 *Cryptanthus* or Earth Star grows wild in rocky fissures, on tree roots or stumps, or on leafy jungle debris, the roots serving mainly to anchor not to nourish. Such plants, which are suitable for growing on logs, are known as terrestrial bromeliads. True or false?

9 Airplane Propellor Plant, Jade Tree, Sickle Plant, Tailor's Patch, Toy Cypress and Scarlet Paintbrush are all common names, used chiefly in America, for plants in which genus of succulents?

10 *Cestrum* hybrids (pictured right), which have sweetly scented flowers borne in clusters, are best grown in the conservatory as they are vigorous and can grow quite tall. In order to thrive, when should these plants be pruned?
(a) Late spring (b) Autumn (c) Late winter

11 *Pandanus* or Screw Pine takes its common name from the spiral arrangement of its shiny, leathery leaves. Why should you take care when handling these leaves?

12 The evergreen house plant commonly known as Croton is much prized for its foliage, which may be oval, oblong or strap-shaped, but which of these phrases best describes its colouring?
(a) Dark green (b) Multi-coloured (c) Silvery

6 Name the Hertfordshire nursery which ceased production in 1983 after some 250 years of business, during which time they had introduced successful citrus varieties to Florida and California.

7 Name the garden designer and writer who presented the popular television series *Gardens By Design*.

8 The Savill Garden, which was devised and planned by Sir Eric Savill in 1932 and greatly enlarged after World War II, lies within which of the Royal Parks?

1 Managed by the National Trust since 1952, these gardens in Wales (shown above) feature the Aviary Terrace, an orangery and a Douglas Fir that is reputed to be the tallest tree in Britain. Which gardens are they?

2 The formal garden at Harewood House is the work of Sir Charles Barry, while the celebrated and prolific 'Capability' Brown was responsible for the landscaping. What was Brown's first name?

3 Which of these British island groups stages an annual 'Floral Island Festival'?
(a) Scilly Isles (b) Channel Islands (c) Shetland Islands

4 Which one of the following men established the *Cyclamen* and Auricula as garden plants, introduced or re-introduced *Hyacinthus* to Europe and is credited with founding the Dutch bulb industry?
(a) L'Obel (b) Clusius (c) Linnaeus

5 Since the end of World War I the Corn Poppy has been accepted in Britain as the flower of remembrance, largely due to the moving poem 'In Flanders Fields'. Who was the creator of these much-quoted verses?
(a) Wilfred Owen (b) Siegfried Sassoon (c) John McRae

9 Which botanist, plant hunter and writer made important botanical journeys to China, Tibet, Burma and Thailand and published, in 1913, *The Land of the Blue Poppy*.

10 What is the name of the garden feature, now chiefly ornamental, that uses concentric hoops of metal to indicate the path of the planets across the heavens?

11 The Victorian writer and critic Percy Lubbock wrote of ". . . a mazy confusion of everything that gleams and glows and exhales a spicery of humming fragrance" in which ". . . everything bloomed tumultuously". What garden feature was he describing?

12 Can you identify the celebrated 17th-century diarist, chemist and writer (pictured right) who experimented with growing many varieties of fruit trees and vines at his 40-hectare (100-acre) garden at Sayes Court, Deptford.

ROUND THIRTEEN

Various alpine plants grow naturally on slopes of rocky detritous eroded from the mountain-sides, which provides good drainage for their roots. This environment can be created in the garden using a deep layer of stone chippings mixed with loam, as shown here. What is such an area called?

6 Which one of the plants listed below would not thrive on a dry sunny bank?
(a) *Heleborus* (b) *Dianthus* (c) *Alyssum*

7 Which of the following plants is not a herbaceous perennial, but an evergreen shrub?
(a) *Phlox* (b) *Solidago* (c) *Kalmia*

8 Which type of underground storage organ consists mainly of fleshy scales and swollen, modified leaf bases on a reduced stem, found in such plants as lilies?

1 *Lactiflora* (pictured above) is just one of the species in the genus of beautiful garden flowers known as *Paeonia*. It blooms from mid to late summer. True or false?

2 'Plum Crazy', 'Brass Band', 'Red Satin' and 'Strawberry Tart' are all F$_1$ varieties of which popular edging, window box and hanging basket plant?

9 What name is given to the genus of plants, suitable for growing on rock gardens, of which London Pride (pictured right) is a popular variety?

3 The common name of the perennial *Nepeta* (shown left) is said to arise from the attraction its fragrance has to a popular domestic animal. What is this name?

10 Which plant is sometimes known as the Flower of Aphrodite, and produces edible flowers from which oil is distilled for use in the production of perfume?

11 This beautiful violet-blue iris (shown left) is an ideal plant for the rockery and the fronts of borders. Its bulbs are criss-crossed with fibres, giving them a netted appearance from which the plant derives what species name?

4 What term is given to a stem joint, sometimes swollen, from which leaves, buds and lateral shoots or branches arise?

5 *Asplenium scolopendrium* is an evergreen fern with strap-like fronds. By which common name is it known?
(a) Sensitive Fern (b) Hart's-tongue Fern (c) Royal Fern

12 Judging from its name, in which areas of the country might *Eryngium maritimum* be expected to thrive?

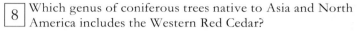

1 Included in the *Prunus* genus of ornamental flowering trees are the cherries (pictured left). Can you name three other fruit trees in this genus.

2 What is the name given to the clear trunk of a tree from ground level to the first branch?

3 *Pyracantha* or Firethorn, which produces attractive white flowers and is often grown as a wall shrub or hedging plant, bears bright berries from September until March. True or false?

4 Despite their names, Mop-head Acacia, Rose Acacia and False Acacia (shown right) do not belong to the *Acacia* genus. What is the correct generic classification?

5 Feather Top, Foxtail Barley and Gardener's Garters are all regularly used names for which type of foliage plant?

6 What is the meaning of the word *sinensis* when used in plant names such as *Wisteria sinensis*?

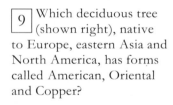

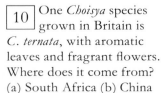

7 Most hollies are unisexual, meaning that a male plant should be grown in the vicinity of the berry-bearing female (pictured left). What is approximately the greatest distance they can be grown apart and still be expected to achieve pollination?
(a) 30 metres (33 yards)
(b) 60 metres (66 yards)
(c) 90 metres (99 yards)

8 Which genus of coniferous trees native to Asia and North America includes the Western Red Cedar?

9 Which deciduous tree (shown right), native to Europe, eastern Asia and North America, has forms called American, Oriental and Copper?

10 One *Choisya* species grown in Britain is *C. ternata*, with aromatic leaves and fragrant flowers. Where does it come from?
(a) South Africa (b) China (c) Mexico

11 What is the name of the popular and generous-sounding hybrid resulting from a cross between *Mahonia japonica* and *M. lomariifolia*?

12 Which one of the following closely related genera is a genus of shrub, rather than a herbaceous perennial?
(a) *Spiraea* (b) *Aruncus* (c) *Filipendula*

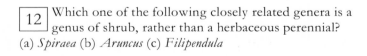

1 It takes over 4000 dried flowers of *Crocus sativus* (pictured right) to produce just 25 grams (one ounce) of a commodity for which the plant was once cultivated in Britain. What is this commodity?

2 Which of the following varieties is the odd one out and why?
(a) 'Ailsa Craig' (b) 'Sturon'
(c) 'Dutch Yellow'

3 'Western Perfection', a purple top, and 'Best of All', a bronze top, are both susceptible to the diseases club root, downy mildew and soft rot. Of which annual winter vegetable are they both varieties?

4 What is the name given to the dense mass of immature flower buds that forms the heads of such vegetables as cauliflower and broccoli?

5 Which fruit (shown left), though closely related to plums, grows more successfully in areas of higher rainfall and less sun, and has a popular dessert and bottling variety called 'Merryweather'?

6 Which plants, grown mainly for their glossy, brightly coloured fruits, make good pot plants and include types such as 'Bull-nosed Red' that are used for culinary purposes?

7 The traditional, ordinary types of greenhouse cucumber, such as 'Butcher's Disease Resistant' and 'Telegraph', will produce a long, smooth crop, but what effect will failure to remove the male flowers have on the taste?

8 Orchards may be found all over Britain in the humblest of cottage gardens and on the grandest country estates, although it is generally accepted that the most productive are to be found south of the River Trent. Which county is sometimes called 'the orchard of England'?

9 The onion (pictured right) belongs to the genus *Allium*, which includes many garden plants and the herb chives. Can you name two other vegetables in this genus?

10 The small, white maggots of *Erioischa brasicae* live in the soil and eat the roots of members of the brassica family. How is this pest better known?

11 The curious old vegetable known as skirret was often grown for its ornamental white flowers and for its giant leaves which often reached 1.2 metres (4 feet) in height. What part of the plant was eaten?

12 Originating in tropical Asia, okra (shown left) can be grown under glass in Britain to produce the sticky green pods that add an exotic touch to soups and stews. To which family of plants does okra belong?

1 What is the generic name of the plant popularly known as Flowering Maple (pictured left), which has hybrid varieties called 'Fireball' and 'Canary Bird'?

2 The vari-coloured leaves of the house plant *Codiaeum variegatum* are responsible for its common name, which has a biblical derivation. What is it?

3 What colour is indicated by the term *erubescens*, in a plant name as in *Philodendron erubescens*?

4 The widely grown climber *Monstera* or Swiss Cheese Plant (shown right) produces roots that grow above the ground and enable the plant to cling to moss poles or other supports. What are these roots called?

5 The popular plant *Solanum capsicastrum*, which produces shiny berries that ripen to a bright orange in winter, is more usually referred to by which name?
(a) Winter Pepper
(b) Winter Cherry
(c) Winter Grape

6 An areole can be defined as a modified side shoot, cushion-like in form with woolly or barbed hairs, from which flowers and off-shoots arise. To which popular family of house plants is the areole unique?

7 *Scindapsus aureus* or Golden Hunter's Robe has leathery, heart-shaped leaves which may best be described by which of the following words?
(a) Green (b) Variegated (c) Glaucous

8 The Oleander needs greenhouse conditions to thrive in most parts of Britain, but around which of the following seas does it occur naturally?
(a) Mediterranean (b) Indian Ocean (c) Aegean Sea

9 What 'heavenly' word features in the common names of certain plants from each of these genera?
(a) *Caladium* (b) *Billbergia*
(c) *Datura*

10 Which is the correct name for this most popular of pot plants (pictured right)?
(a) *Celosia* (b) *Calceolaria*
(c) *Cineraria*

11 *Lithops* plants of the hot, sunny desert regions are similar in appearance to the pebbles among which they grow. How are these plants often known?

12 Best grown indoors in moist and humid conditions, *Anthurium scherzerianum* is an ideal house plant for the kitchen or bathroom. Its common name is derived from the resemblance of its large, exotic-looking flowers to which, equally large and exotic bird.

1 The National Trust gardens at Bodnant in Wales (shown above), home of Lord Aberconway, are among the finest gardens in Britain. In which county is Bodnant?

2 What name is given to the blanket planting of masses of flowers, usually in formal geometric beds, that was popular in Victorian times and is still much used by local council Parks Departments?

3 In the gardens of which Cambridgeshire Abbey is the Emperors' Walk lined with the busts of Roman rulers as well as a marble copy of Bernini's 'David'?

4 The name of which horticulturalist and property developer is widely remembered for the compost formula first marketed some 35 years after his death?

5 What name was given to the heated glass house found in many Victorian kitchen gardens in which tropical and exotic plants were raised?

6 Which 18th-century gardener and plant hunter was honoured in the botanical name of the genus that is commonly known as Jew's Mallow?
(a) Johann Zinn (b) William Kerr (c) Pierre Magnol

7 The gardens at Keddleston Hall in Derbyshire include a triple-arched bridge, a bath house and an orangery by which famous designer?

8 Which early American plant hunter founded his country's first botanic gardens and introduced several species, including *Magnolia grandiflora*, to Britain?

9 Can you name the Frenchman, born in 1613, who was responsible for the creation of the gardens at Versailles, Chantilly and Vaux-le-Vicomte?

10 Vistors to Chenies Manor in Buckinghamshire, Hatfield House in Hertfordshire and Chatsworth House in Derbyshire could all expect to see fine mazes. True or false?

11 Which Irish-born advocate of cottage-style gardens and lifelong friend to Gertrude Jekyll founded *The Garden* magazine in 1871?
(a) Edwin Luytens (b) William Robinson (c) Charles Dickens

12 In many country house gardens a line of deciduous trees often had their branches trimmed and interlaced in order to link together each tree. What name is given to this feature (pictured above)?
(a) Palisade (b) Arcade (c) Colonnade

ROUND FOURTEEN

Rambling roses (shown here) and climbing roses, some of which are true climbing species while others are sports of bush roses, are both suited to scrambling over almost any permanent structure. A climbing rose should be pruned during its dormant season, but when is the correct time to prune a rambling rose?

1 *Asphodeline lutea* or King's Spear (pictured right), mentioned in the writings of Pliny, was grown by the Ancient Greeks for its thick, edible roots. It originates in the Himalayas. True or false?

2 The Windflower is a hardy, herbaceous plant belonging to the same family as the Buttercup. What is its generic name?

3 Carnations are much admired for their brightly coloured blooms, but which of the following background colours is common to the varieties 'Dainty Lady', 'Forest Treasure' and 'Bryony Lisa'?
(a) Yellow (b) Pink (c) White

4 Although the original Crystal Palace was destroyed by fire in 1936, it is still commemorated in many gardens today in a popular blue-flowered, bronze-leafed variety of which summer-bedding and edging plant?

5 Suitable for the rock garden or as edging to beds and borders, *Armeria maritima* (shown left) is, as its name suggests, quite at home on coastal cliff tops. What is its common name?

6 A traditional method of cleaning up *Cortaderia* or Pampas Grass was to set fire to it towards the end of winter. True or false?

7 The *Heuchera* or Coral Flower produces plumes of tiny, bell-shaped flowers in a variety of shades of pink and red. Is it evergreen or deciduous?

8 The yellow-flowered perennial herbaceous genus known to most gardeners as Solomon's Seal is known by which of the following botanical names?
(a) *Polystichum* (b) *Polygonum* (c) *Polygonatum*

9 A plant that occurs naturally in the mountain area between the tree line and the permanent snow line can be correctly described as a what?

10 Often used as carpet bedding or in window boxes, it is a small plant which produces white or pink, button-like or double-daisy flowers and is related to the Common Daisy. Can you supply its generic name?

11 *Iris laevigata* is a true water and waterside plant happiest in up to 15 centimetres (6 inches) of water. Although there is a white-flowered variety (pictured above), what is the usual colour of the species?

12 The border or rock-garden plant *Lysimachia* or Loosestrife belongs to the same family as which one of the following flowers?
(a) *Primula* (b) *Potentilla* (c) Peony

1 *Cordyline* is a genus of palm-like shrubs and trees of which *C. australis*, as its name suggests, originates in Australia. What is the country of origin of *C. indivisa*?

2 Which tree may be Sessile, Pendunculate, Cork or Red? (a) Plane (b) Beech (c) Oak

3 The leaves of *Rosa eglanteria* (shown above) are covered with glands that emit a sweet, pungent fragrance which gives rise to one of its common names, Sweet Briar. What is the other?

4 What can be defined as a thread-like organ of a climbing plant which twines arounds a support or attaches itself to a surface by means of terminal suckers?

5 *Solanum crispum* or Chilean Potato Tree, a semi-evergreen climber producing flowers similar in appearance to the Deadly Nightshade, is related to the edible potato. True or false?

6 The deciduous, ornamental tree *Tilia* makes a handsome specimen tree for large gardens and in the past was much used to line avenues. Its flower nectar is a great attraction for bees. What is its common name?

7 The deciduous shrub *Exochorda racemosa* or Pearl Bush will produce its white flowers throughout August and September. True or false?

8 The deciduous, spring-flowering shrub *Forsythia*, sometimes used as hedging, will produce a profusion of flowers which open before the leaves emerge. What colour are these flowers?

9 *Enkianthus campanulatus* has bell-shaped flowers and brilliant red autumn foliage. From which country was it introduced to Britain in 1880 by the Veitch family?

10 The genus *Rubus* contains around 250 hardy, erect or scrambling, usually prickly shrubs, such as Blackberry, Thimbleberry and Bramble. Are the plants in this genus evergreen, semi-evergreen or deciduous?

11 The mahogany-brown seeds of the massive, spreading tree *Aesculus hippocastanum* (pictured left) provide food for deer and cattle, as well as entertainment for children. By what name are these seeds popularly known?

12 It was once the custom to mask any lack of domestic hygiene by laying the woody perennial Southernwood or Lad's Love on the floor because of the pleasant aroma created when the plant was crushed underfoot. Under which generic heading is this herb listed?

1 Attractive to butterflies, this herb (shown above), which will make a good low hedge in the ornamental kitchen garden, may be infused to make a medicinal tea and its young leaves are often added to salads or dried and used in potpourris. What is its common name?

2 What is the name of the condition common in the peach, in which the green of a leaf is replaced by pale green, yellow or white and which results from a viral disease or mineral deficiency?

3 'Malling Admiral', 'Malling Delight' and 'Malling Jewel' are all popular varieties of a hardy, deciduous cane fruit native to most countries in Europe. Which of these is it?
(a) Strawberry (b) Raspberry (c) Loganberry

4 Tomatoes first arrived in Europe in the 16th century, brought by missionaries from Central America. What colour was the earliest variety?

5 Pumpkins (shown left), marrows and squashes all belong to the gourd family. True or false?

6 The mild-flavoured onion 'White Lisbon' is most commonly grown as a salad or bunching onion, but what is the most popular use of the variety 'Paris Silverskin'?

7 Towards the end of the 19th century most large garden estates had special buildings devoted to the production of such delights as 'Smooth-leaved Cayenne', 'Queens' and 'Charlotte Rothschild'. Of which fruit were they varieties?

8 Identify the odd one out of the following fruit varieties in that it is a plum rather than a peach.
(a) 'Duke of York' (b) 'Czar' (c) 'Peregrine'

9 Which salad plant includes a curled-leaf group known as staghorns as well as batavians with plain leaves?

10 The leaves of the herb *Melissa officinalis* (pictured right) have a lemony fragrance, and are used as a flavouring for salads. How is this herb popularly known?

11 What structure can be described as a simple, dry, indehiscent, one-seeded fruit with a hard, woody shell?

12 Sometimes called the Turnip Cabbage, this vegetable is grown for its swollen stem which appears above ground level and has varieties known as 'Purple Delicatesse' and 'Primavera'. What vegetable is it?

1 The bulbous, late winter-flowering and sweetly fragrant *Freesia* (shown left) is often grown in pots in a conservatory or as a house plant. To which of the following countries is it indigenous?
(a) Peru (b) South Africa (c) Japan

2 What is the common name of the popular foliage house plant *Schefflera actinophylla*, which is derived from the arrangement of its large, shiny leaves?

3 Great care should be taken when cutting any part of the *Dieffenbachia* as its poisonous sap may render a person speechless if enough of it goes onto the tongue. As a result, what is the common name of this species?

4 *Schlumbergera truncata* or Crab Cactus (pictured right) has freely branching, jointed stems and produces a spectacular display of flowers in shades of red, pink, white or purple. At what time of year are the flowers produced?

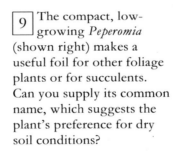

5 Can you identify the erect, semi-climbing foliage plant that is commonly known as Tree Ivy or Aralia Ivy, and results from a cross, as its botanical name suggests, between two distinct genera?

6 Provided that all other environmental conditions are suitable, the orchid genera *Cattleya*, *Oncidium* and *Miltonia* require a minimum night temperature of 21°C (70°F) to survive in Britain. True or false?

7 The trailing creeper *Callisia elegans*, which is similar and related to the *Tradescantia*, has a green and white upper surface to its leaves. What colour is the underside?

8 If given sufficient heat, *Polianthes tuberosa* can be induced to produce its fragrant, white flowers at any time. True or false?

9 The compact, low-growing *Peperomia* (shown right) makes a useful foil for other foliage plants or for succulents. Can you supply its common name, which suggests the plant's preference for dry soil conditions?

10 *Sarracenias* are a genus of carnivorous bog plants. What term is used to describe such plants, which offer their prey a drink before digesting them?

11 Two of the following plants have a bushy habit, but which is the odd one out in that it is a trailer?
(a) *Clivia* (b) *Callisia* (c) *Streptocarpus*

12 This genus of popular indoor succulents, which have beautifully marked leaves and tubular flowers, includes species nicknamed Felt Bush and Pussy Ears, and miniature forms called 'Tom Thumb' and 'Vulcan'. What is the botanical name of the genus?

7 Trebah Gardens in Cornwall, Hodnet Hall in Shropshire and the Beth Chatto Gardens in Essex all possess particularly fine examples of the use of water as a garden feature. True or false?

8 Name the 16th-century Frenchman, botanist and physician to James I after whom Linnaeus named a genus of some 200 plants of the Campanulaceae family.

1 Which Buckinghamshire house features a huge, French, 17th-century aviary (pictured above) on one of the parterres, bird and animal sculptures on the lawns and free-flying macaws overhead?

2 Which well-known writer and presenter of gardening and other programmes for television regularly recounts his 'tales' in *Gardeners' World* magazine?

3 The grounds of Sizergh Castle in Cumbria include many fascinating features, such as lakes, ponds and conifers, but their principal attraction was created in 1926 by the Ambleside nursery firm of T. R. Hayes and covers around one square kilometre (a quarter of an acre). What is it?

4 By what name did the Victorians know a decorative seat surrounded by a framework of wooden poles clothed in such fragrant climbers as *Jasminum officinale* and the rose 'Gloire de Dijon'?

5 The gardens of the hotel that was founded by the Scot William Reid in 1887 have since become famous throughout the world. On which island in the Atlantic will you find Reid's hotel?

6 The Ulster gardens of Castlewellan, Rowallane and Mount Stewart are all within which county?
(a) Armagh (b) Antrim (c) County Down

9 Which Victorian lady, whose husband founded Britain's first garden magazine, wrote widely on rock-work and published *Gardening for Ladies* in 1840?

10 Trellis-work or lattice frames make attractive and versatile additions to almost any garden. What is the name, originating in France, by which this type of ornamentation is also known.

11 With which flower is the nurseryman and plant breeder Harry Wheatcroft most closely associated?

12 These large, impressive gardens (shown below) were created in North Yorkshire in 1948 by the Northern Horticultural Society as the northern counterpart of Wisley. Can you name them?

ROUND
FIFTEEN

The compact, hardy, evergreen shrub pictured
here has leathery leaves and produces waxy
flowers, resembling those of Lily-of-the-valley,
in spring. It requires lime-free soil and grows
best in a partially shaded situation. Formerly
known as *Andromeda*, this genus is now listed
under what botanical name?

1 *Lysichiton* or Skunk Cabbage (shown above) is a plant for the bog garden, grown for its handsome foliage and attractively shaped flowers. Which of the following terms refers to blooms of this shape?
(a) Floret (b) Spathe (c) Blade

2 What word describes plants that die after flowering and seeding, in particular annuals and biennials but also perennials which grow for some years before flowering profusely and then dying?

3 The bulb *Erythronium dens-canis* (pictured left) is a graceful plant suitable for a rock garden or a container. What is its common name, which includes a translation of part of its botanical name.

4 What name is given to the sweet liquid secreted by some plants to attract insects that aid pollination?

5 Which of the following genera can be successfully grown in an alkaline soil?
(a) *Lapageria* (b) *Fuchsia* (c) *Camellia*

6 What common name is given to the summer to autumn-flowering, herbaceous perennial *Aster novi-belgii*?

7 Most of the mainly half-hardy *Phormiums* may be grown outside only in the south of England, but to which country in the southern hemisphere are they indigenous?

8 Is the *Cyclamen* (shown right), which is usually grown for its attractive, pendent flowers, annual, biennial or perennial?

9 Match the plants with the appropriate food storage systems.
(i) Lily (ii) Bearded Iris
(iii) Dahlia
(a) Bulb (b) Rhizome
(c) Tuber

10 The common name for *Solidago*, the genus of hardy, summer- and autumn- flowering, border and rock garden plants is Golden Chain. True or false?

11 What is the common name of the plant that thrives in Australia and Madeira and is also the national floral emblem of South Africa?

12 The Sea Lavender or *Limonium* (pictured left), popular for drying as an everlasting plant, is still often referred to by what former generic name?

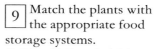

1 The hardy, deciduous, loosely climbing shrub *Jasminum nudiflorum* produces striking, bright yellow flowers either singly or in small clusters. By which of the following names is it commonly known?
(a) Common White Jasmine (b) Primrose Jasmine (c) Winter Jasmine

2 What does the word 'Fastigiata' as in *Taxus baccata* 'Fastigiata' reveal about the plant's shape?

3 What name is given to the main anchoring root of a plant, particularly a tree?

4 The deciduous shrub Guelder Rose (shown below) grows wild in Britain, bearing scented white flowers in May and June followed by transluscent red berries in autumn. To which genus of around 200 widely distributed species does it belong?

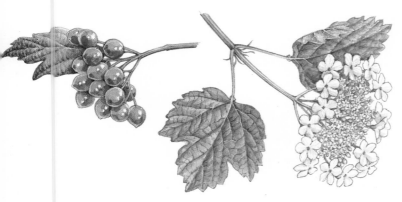

5 The widely grown ornamental and timber tree *Pinus sylvestris* may reach heights in excess of 9 metres (30 feet). What is its common name?

6 Name the type of propagation in which a stem is induced to root by pegging it down into the soil while it is still attached to the parent plant?

7 The wood of the tree *Buxus sempervirens* was originally used in the manufacture of musical instruments, and another item in everyday use, from which its common name is derived. What is this name?

8 Species in the Cupressaceae family (cypresses) of hardy, evergreen conifers are native to North America, Japan and Formosa. From which of these areas does the commonly grown *Chamaecyparis lawsoniana* (pictured left) originate?

9 'Picasso', 'Regensburg', 'Maestro' and 'Uncle Walter' are all varieties of which widely grown shrub?
(a) Rose (b) Clematis (c) Rhododendron

10 The shrubs *Syringa*, *Escallonia* and *Tamarix* are all suitable for growing as hedging, but which is the odd one out in that it is the only genus that includes mainly evergreen as well as a few deciduous species?

11 What is the common name of *Fraxinus*, which produces a winged fruit after flowering?

12 To which tree that produces fruit used in preserves, do these attractive flowers (shown right) belong?

1 Vegetables such as turnips and parsnips are grown for their edible roots. What is the name of the edible part of the potato (pictured right)?

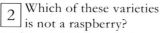

2 Which of these varieties is not a raspberry?
(a) 'Zeva' (b) 'Grandee'
(c) 'Norfolk Giant'

3 What term is applied to a fruit tree that is pruned to a single main stem with short side shoots?

4 Courgette or Baby Marrow is a member of the squash family, but by what name is it normally referred to in North America, reflecting that continent's ethnic diversity?

5 *Carum carvi* (shown left) is a biennial herb whose seeds are used as a flavouring for cakes, cheeses and salads and, commercially, the liqueur Kümmel. By what common name is this herb known?

6 The fruit tree *Cydonia oblonga* produces acid-tasting, strongly aromatic, yellow fruit, used in preserves, and is generally available in only two varieties, 'Portugal' and 'Vranja'. What is its common name?

7 Greenhouse varieties of melon such as 'Charentais', 'Sweetheart' and 'Tiger' require a minimum temperature of 27°C (70°F). True or false?

8 By sowing the varieties 'Pixie', 'Hawke', 'January King' and 'Best of All' it is possible to cut this popular vegetable all year round. What is it?

9 Link the following types of vegetable with their appropriate varieties:
(i) Pea (ii) Radish (iii) Potato
(a) 'Meteor' (b) 'Epicure' (c) 'French Breakfast'

10 Which vegetable, a relative of the tomato, requires similar growing conditions and has popular varieties called 'Yellow Lantern' and 'Gold Star'?

11 This hardy, deciduous tree produces round, hard but fleshy fruit (pictured right), which can be eaten raw when it has become 'bletted' or over-ripe, but is more usually

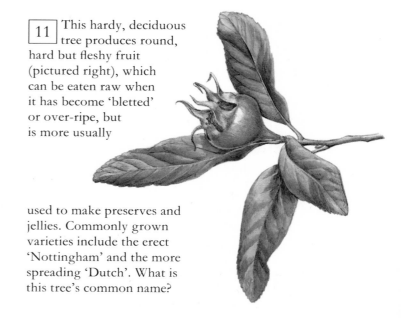

used to make preserves and jellies. Commonly grown varieties include the erect 'Nottingham' and the more spreading 'Dutch'. What is this tree's common name?

12 Which of the following vegetable varieties is the odd one out and why?
(a) 'Boltardy' (b) 'Monodet' (c) 'The Prince'

1 This striking conservatory shrub (shown above) is sometimes classified as *Brugmansia*, but under what generic name is it more likely to be listed?

2 Although the petal lobes of *Thunbergia* may be seen in a variety of colours, all forms have a deep chocolate-brown 'eye', giving rise to the plant's more usual name. What is it?

3 Which of the following plants is not a member of the same botanical family as the hyacinth?
(a) *Aspidistra* (b) *Scilla* (c) *Jacaranda*

4 Which of the following terms cannot be accurately used to describe the *Rhoicissus*?
(a) Tender (b) Climbing (c) Deciduous

5 What botanical name was formerly given to the palm *Chrysalidocarpus lutescens* with its delicate, arching fronds on clusters of yellow, reed-like stems?

6 What French term is used for an arrangement made by placing cut flowers in a pot of indoor foliage plants?

7 Produced from a 0.9–1.2 metre (3–4 foot) high evergreen shrub, the fragrant white blooms of Cape Jasmine are popular with flower arrangers and were once common as buttonholes. How is this plant better known?

8 Of the genus *Scirpus* or Bulrush the only species generally grown indoors is *S. cernuus*. Which of the following is most descriptive of its habit?
(a) Grass-like (b) Climber (c) Tree-like

9 The *Rebutia* or Crown Cactus (pictured right) produces an impressive display of fiery red blooms which arise both from the main plant and from its offsets. Of the cacti grown indoors, this is one of the first to flower each year. True or false?

10 The small palm *Chamaedorea elegans* has acquired the common name of Lounge Palm. True or false?

11 *Mandevilla sanderi* (shown left), which was formerly known as *Dipladenia sanderi*, is grown mainly for its showy, trumpet-shaped, rose-pink flowers. This plant has a climbing habit of growth. True or false?

12 What term is used to describe the feathery, compound leaves of ferns, palms and certain other foliage plants?

1 In which English county would you find the beautiful gardens at Knightshayes Court that feature this pool garden (pictured above)?

2 The first Horticultural Society Fête was held at Chiswick in 1827 and the society became 'Royal' in 1861, but in which of these years was it founded?
(a) 1798 (b) 1804 (c) 1826

3 The first British rose to be patented was produced by the Dickson Nurseries and named appropriately 'Grandpa Dickson'. Where in the British Isles was this rose bred?
(a) Glamorgan (b) County Down (c) Strathclyde

4 Name the style of container that is usually planted with citrus or Bay trees, and which derives its name from the palace gardens in France where it was used to emphasize the patterns of the parterres.

5 The gardens created by Thomas Simpson at Compton Acres represent a number of countries, including Italy, Japan and England. In which county is Compton Acres?

6 Which 18th-century English dramatist and architect, assisted by Nicholas Hawksmoor, designed both Blenheim Palace and Castle Howard?

7 Many hedges in larger gardens are trimmed at an incline rather than vertically to improve their appearance and encourage growth at the base. Which word describes this type of clipping?
(a) Layering (b) Battering (c) Scalloping

8 Name the eminent woman gardener, writer and holder of the Victoria Medal of Honour from the Royal Horticultural Society whose garden at Elmstead Market in Essex includes a wide variety of plants ranging from Mediterranean sun lovers to waterside bog plants.

9 In which Buckinghamshire garden is William Kent's Temple of the British Worthies with busts of Queen Elizabeth I, Shakespeare, Bacon, Milton and others?
(a) Blenheim (b) Hatfield House (c) Stowe

10 Born in 1716, this son of a farmer began working as a gardener at the age of 16 and went on to become one of the most prolific and influential landscape designers of all time (shown right). His creations include Longleat, Syon Park, Chatsworth and Blenheim. Who was he?

11 Designed by Joseph Paxton, it took four years to build and was, at the time of its completion in 1840, the largest greenhouse in the world. In 1919 it was blown up by the 9th Duke of Devonshire. What was it?

12 Winter Jasmine, Winter Honeysuckle and Bleeding Heart were all introduced to this country as a result of expeditions to the Orient by a plantsman whose name is commemorated in a rhododendron species he collected from the wild. Can you name him?

ROUND SIXTEEN

A cave-like structure, sometimes natural but usually artificial, it was often lined with shells and pebbles. The inclusion of a water feature created an ideal environment for ferns and mosses. An example at Hever Castle (pictured here) is set within its own garden of moisture-loving plants. What is being described?

1 The hardy, evergreen Soft Shield Fern (shown left), which occurs naturally in many parts of Britain, is in the same genus as the Christmas Fern, Sword Fern and Japanese Holly Fern. To which of the following genera do they all belong?
(a) *Adiantum* (b) *Davallia* (c) *Polystichum*

2 *Gunnera manicata* produces majestic, dark green foliage and is ideal as a pool-side plant although its crowns need winter protection. From which part of the world does it originate?
(a) South America (b) China (c) New Zealand

3 What name is given to the green pigment in the leaves and stems of plants?

4 The *Agapanthus* is popular as a cut flower or, dried, for winter decoration. What is its common name, reflecting the continent from which it originates?

5 The silvery seed pods of *Lunaria* are useful as indoor decoration. By what name are these biennial and perennial plants better known?

6 The hardy perennial *Sisyrinchium* (pictured right) needs a sunny position in which to produce its flowers, but where does it prefer to have its roots?
(a) In boggy ground
(b) In well-drained soil
(c) In water

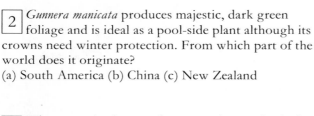

7 *Leucojum* or Snowflake is sometimes confused with *Galanthus* or Snowdrop. In addition to its flowers being larger and more rounded in appearance, what feature of its six petals makes it more easily distinguishable?

8 Which genus of hardy, bulbous plants related to the Hyacinth, and sometimes known as Grape Hyacinth, is useful not only for borders, rock gardens and edging but also for use in cut flower arrangements?

9 A good plant for a rock garden, the low-growing, hardy perennial *Oxalis acetosella* forms neat tufts of pale green, shamrock-like leaves, and produces white funnel-shaped flowers. What is its common name?

10 The tall, erect stems of the hardy perennial *Aconitum* (shown left) make it an ideal plant for the back of a herbaceous border. What is its 'ecclesiastical' common name, which it owes to its unusually shaped flowers?
(a) Monkshood (b) Bishop's Mitre (c) Pope's Cap

11 The perennial *Potentilla* or Cinquefoil belongs to the same plant family as which one of the following?
(a) Buttercup (b) Rose (c) Petunia

12 Which commonly seen flower, with species popularly known as Iceland and Oriental, is known by the botanical name *Papaver*?

1 *Erica cinerea* (pictured left) is one of a large genus of plants grown for their flowers and mat-forming, evergreen foliage. Is this particular species better known as Dorset Heather or Bell Heather?

2 The deciduous shrub *Amelanchier canadensis*, which has autumn leaf tints and white, star-shaped flowers, produces edible berries that are often eaten in desserts. True or false?

3 The hardy perennial *Hypericum* or St John's Wort includes the golden-flowered *H. calycinum*, popularly known as Aaron's Beard and by what other common name?

4 If male and female forms are grown together, the shrub *Hippophae rhamnoides* will produce an autumn crop of orange berries (shown right). What colour are its flowers?

5 What name is given to the main stem or stems of a tree or shrub that serves to extend the existing branch system?

6 The two related genera of shrubs *Cytisus* and *Genista* have which popular name in common?

7 Two of the three varieties listed below are climbing roses, the other is a miniature bush. Which is it? (a) 'Mermaid' (b) 'Angela Rippon' (c) 'Handel'

8 What unpleasant characteristic is common to privets, junipers, ivies and hollies?

9 Maples (pictured above) are trees and shrubs grown mainly for their ornamental foliage and whose leaf is featured on the national flag of Canada. Under what botanical heading is the genus listed?

10 The tree *Liquidambar styraciflua* is generally grown for its ridged bark and maple-like leaves which turn orange, red or purple in autumn. The amber resin exuded by the tree is the basis of both its botanical and common name. How is it popularly known?

11 *Drimys* is a genus of shrubs grown for their foliage and star-shaped flowers with one species commonly known as Winter's Bark. Are they evergreen or deciduous?

12 *Phygelius* is a genus comprising only two species, both of which flower from July to October. Should these shrubs be grown in sun or shade?

1 Before the advent of dwarfing rootstocks, fruit trees grew to considerable heights and had to be shaped and trimmed with long-handled pruners. Several different types were evolved including shear-action (shown right), pulley-action and parrot-bill. What were these pruners called?

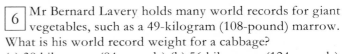

2 In the 16th century fruit and vegetables were often grown in elaborate arrangements of decorative beds that were frequently edged by a low hedge of clipped box or a pattern of pathways. What French word is applied to such an ornamental kitchen garden today?

3 'Riesling Sylvaner' and 'Siegerrebe' are both outdoor varieties of which climbing shrub, grown for its fruit, which is also cultivated under glass in Britain?

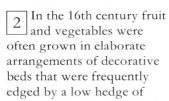

4 *Levisticum officinale* (pictured left) is widely grown for use in salads or, when dried, as a flavouring for soups and stews. How is it more commonly known?

5 'China Rose', 'Black Spanish' and 'Scarlet Globe' are all varieties of radish. Two are large winter forms. Which of the three is the smaller, summer type?

6 Mr Bernard Lavery holds many world records for giant vegetables, such as a 49-kilogram (108-pound) marrow. What is his world record weight for a cabbage?
(a) 38 kilograms (84 pounds) (b) 56 kilograms (124 pounds) (c) 69 kilograms (154 pounds)

7 Can you name the straight and often shallow furrow in which seeds, usually vegetables, are sown outdoors?

8 In Victorian times which crop was raised in a glass tube or long wooden box to make it grow uniformly straight?
(a) Rhubarb (b) Cucumber (c) Leek

9 The commonly cultivated varieties of this deciduous shrub (shown left) will, when grown under suitable conditions, produce a good fruit crop from August to October. True or false?

10 Approximately how long after sowing swede seeds can the first crop be harvested?
(a) 8–10 weeks (b) 10–15 weeks (c) 20–24 weeks

11 *Actinidia chinensis* is a vigorous, ornamental climber with dark green, heart-shaped leaves and clusters of cream-white flowers. What name is generally given to the edible fruit which follows these flowers?

12 *Sinapis alba* and *Lepidium sativum* may be something of a mouthful, but how are they more commonly known when used in their seedling stage as salad vegetables or for sandwich fillings?

1 *Sedum morganianum* is a greenhouse or conservatory species of an attractive succulent and makes a good basket plant. By which of the following names is it not generally known?
(a) Beaver's Tail (b) Bird's Tail (c) Donkey's Tail

2 The unusual flowers of this South American plant (pictured right) were said to have been used by Roman Catholic priests to illustrate the story of the Crucifixion to the Indian tribes they converted to Christianity. What is the common name of this popular conservatory or house plant?

3 *Schizostylis coccinea* makes an ideal pot plant for the conservatory and, although slightly tender, can also be grown outside in a sheltered, sunny position. At what time of year does it produce its beautiful flowers?

4 The bushy *Bassia scoparia*, which is more widely known as *Kochia scoparia*, derives its common name of Burning Bush from its vibrant, deep red autumn colouring. Is this colour provided by the flowers, fruit or foliage?

5 The tooth-edged leaves of *Faucaria* (shown left) are responsible for its popular name of Tiger's Jaw, and its large, yellow, daisy-like flowers appear in autumn. In which of the following countries does this plant originate?
(a) Mexico (b) South Africa (c) China

6 The house plants *Browallia*, *Exacum* and *Campanula* will all produce bright yellow flowers. True or false?

7 Sword Brake, Trembling Fern and Ribbon Fern are all common names applied to species or cultivars of which genus of widely grown house plants?

8 *Rhoeo* (pictured right) is particularly attractive for the unusual, boat-like involucre which holds the flowers. Which of the following is not one of its common names?
(a) Boat Lily (b) Moses-in-the-rushes (c) Three-men-in-a-boat

9 The plants *Aphelandra*, *Pachystachys* and *Allamanda* will all produce flowers of which colour?

10 A conservatory in which a minimum night temperature of 7°C (45°F) was maintained would be an appropriate environment for which one of the following?
(a) *Saintpaulia* (b) *Canna* (c) *Brunfelsia*

11 What is the botanical name of the house plant commonly known as Painted Drop Tongue, which is grown for its ornamental foliage, and which includes the popular form 'Silver Queen'?

12 *Maranta leuconeura erythroneura* is a variety from Brazil with ovate, upright leaves. The unusual patterning on these leaves is the source of which of the following common names?
(a) Snakeskin Plant (b) Herringbone Plant (c) Zig-zag Plant

1 Of which Somerset garden, partly replanned by Vita Sackville-West in 1931 and now administered by the National Trust, did Gertrude Jekyll write in 1904 "... it is all extremely correct, stately ... dare one say, a trifle dull"?

2 The NCCPG plays a vital role in protecting and conserving a wide range of plant species. Which organization is represented by these initials?

3 The gardens at Blickling Hall (shown above) in Norfolk are often wrongly attributed to Humphry Repton although his son John may well have been responsible for the orangery. To what period does the hall itself belong?
(a) Jacobean (b) Tudor (c) Elizabethan

4 The original gardens at Rousham House at Steeple Aston in Oxfordshire were the work of Charles Bridgeman and feature a straight avenue, rectangular ponds and winding paths leading down to which river?
(a) Derwent (b) Severn (c) Cherwell

5 The gardens at Sheffield Park were originally designed by 'Capability' Brown, but which 19th-century landscape artist was brought in by the third earl to enrich the lake and valley?
(a) James Pulham (b) Charles Bridgeman (c) Henry Wise

6 The showpiece of the annual Chelsea Flower Show is the massive Grand Marquee said to be the largest in the world. What area does it cover?
(a) 0.4 hectares (1 acre) (b) 0.8 hectares (2 acres)
(c) 1.4 hectares (3.5 acres)

7 They founded their first nursery in 1832 in Exeter, sent more than 20 plant hunters around the world, three of their number died tragically young and the business finally closed in 1914. Can you name this remarkable family?

8 Can you name the former head gardener who presented the restoration of the garden at Chilton Foliat in the popular television series *The Victorian Kitchen Garden*?

9 What is the name of the horticultural writer and owner of Great Dixter in East Sussex who since 1963 has contributed a regular column to *Country Life* magazine under the heading 'In My Garden'?

10 The Iris is reputed to be named after the Greek goddess of the same name, but of which of the following was she the goddess?
(a) The flower (b) The rainbow (c) The stream

11 Name the substance made by mixing clay with lime which is spread over light soil to improve its structure?

12 As gateposts began to be replaced by brick and masonry pillars they were often topped by fluted urns, balls or pineapples (pictured right). What were these decorations called?

ROUND SEVENTEEN

The cactus family falls into two groups, one being native to the rainforests of the New World, the other thriving in the hot, arid conditions of the deserts. The latter group, unlike most plants, are well suited to the dry, centrally heated rooms found in many homes. Can you identify the desert species shown here?

1 When it was introduced into this country in 1924 this spectacular plant (pictured above) aroused a great deal of interest because of its colour. Can you give either its botanical or common name.

2 The *Alstroemeria* is native to which part of the world, as reflected in the plant's common name?
(a) South America (b) South China (c) South Africa

3 Name the drug used in the treatment of human heart conditions that is derived from the tall, majestic Foxglove (shown right), and which is also the plant's generic name.

4 Which of the following terms is applied to a shield-shaped leaf in which the stalk is inserted near to or at the centre of the blade, rather than at the margin, as in such plants as Canary Creeper?
(a) Dentate (b) Palmate
(c) Peltate

5 In 17th-century Europe the bulbs of rare types of which now common garden plant were exchanged for houses, coaches and even farms?

6 Which of the genera listed below is comprised of the greatest number of species?
(a) *Phormium* (b) *Ipomoea* (c) *Gladiolus*

7 What is the name given to a layer of organic matter applied to the soil in order to conserve moisture, protect roots and enrich the soil?

8 *Aubrieta, Dianthus* and *Sedum* are all suitable plants for growing in a rock garden. True or false?

9 What is the generic name of this popular plant (pictured right), which is ideal for growing in a window box?

10 *Tropaeolum majus* is a hardy, twining climber grown mainly for its brightly coloured flowers, but its leaves may also be used in salads. By what name is this plant more usually known?

11 The daisy-like flowers of the *Scabious* or Pincushion Flower, though excellent for cutting, are susceptible to powdery mildew. True or false?

12 Which of the following would not be suitable as a pool-side or marginal plant?
(a) *Astilbe* (b) *Iris* (c) *Dianthus*

1 Trees of the larch family, including the European Larch and the Japanese Larch (shown left), differ from most other conifers in that they are deciduous. True or false?

2 What name is given to the clipping of trees or shrubs into geometric or fanciful shapes?

3 Members of the hardy *Deutzia* genus of shrubs, which bear white, pink or purple flowers, prefer to be planted in deep shade. True or false?

4 The common name of the deciduous flowering shrub *Philadelphus* is suggested by the fragrance of its white, cup-shaped flowers. What is this name?

5 Can you give the botanical name of this genus of small to medium-sized deciduous, sweetly scented shrubs (pictured right), which is also the name of one of the nymphs of Greek mythology?

6 Which very fast-growing trees, effective as windbreaks or screens, have species known as White, Lombardy, Manchester, and Western Balsam?

7 Grown as a specimen shrub or planted in a shrub border, this upright, spring-flowering plant includes single-flowered varieties such as the fragrant 'Blue Hyacinth', the white-bloomed 'Vestale' and the lilac-blue, scented 'Firmament'. What plant is it?

8 The Sycamore or *Acer pseudoplatanus* has been introduced to many parts of Europe and is now widely naturalized. It is able to spread quickly and easily by means of its twirling, winged seeds (shown left). What are these seeds called?

9 What colour are the flowers of the deciduous, fast-growing shrub *Fremontodendron californicum*?

10 Chiefly grown as a specimen tree in mild areas of Britain, the European or Chusan Palm (pictured right) is a hardier tree than the native European Dwarf Fan Palm, and will survive fairly severe frosts. In which country does it originate?
(a) China (b) Chile
(c) New Zealand

11 If a plant name includes the Latin word 'Aurea', as in *Chamaecyparis obtusa* 'Nana Aurea', what colour would you expect the flowers or foliage to be?

12 What term describes plants that have a woody base but whose terminal shoots may die back in winter?

1 Which of the following statements is incorrect? The most suitable areas for growing apples (shown right) in Britain are those:
(a) South of the River Trent
(b) Above altitudes of 120 metres (400 feet)
(c) Not exposed to wind or salt-laden spray

2 'Sutton's Perfection' and 'Martha Washington' are varieties of which vegetable that is normally first cropped in the second year after planting?

3 What name is given to the mound of soil and straw or bracken in which root crops such as potatoes are stored?

4 What vegetable, of which the variety 'Citadel' should reach the peak of its cropping at Christmas, is best picked when the lower buttons are the size of walnuts?

5 'Bigarreau Napoleon', 'Frogmore Early' and 'Morello' are all varieties of sweet cherry (pictured left). True or false?

6 'Lancer', 'Keepsake' and 'Careless' will all produce a tasty fruit crop from late May to August. What are they?

7 Name the most common cause of maggoty apples, whose caterpillars feed off the fruit during July and August, leaving the affected fruit in late summer, and over-wintering in cocoons attached to loose bark or tree ties.

8 Which vegetable includes the varieties 'Kundulus', which is suitable for stony and heavy soil, and 'Autumn King', which is a good all-rounder for the average garden?

9 'Bloomsdale' is a summer variety, 'Broad-leaved Prickly' is a winter variety and the half-hardy 'New Zealand' is not strictly a true variety. Which vegetable, grown for its succulent leaves, is being described?

10 *Agaricus bisporus* (shown left) is grown commercially in almost every country in the world, but in which of these centuries was it first cultivated?
(a) 16th (b) 18th (c) 20th

11 Which perennial, thought to be a 19th-century cross between the cultivated blackberry and the raspberry, produces oblong, dull, claret-coloured fruit in July and August on shoots of the previous season's growth?

12 Despite being banned by Henry VIII as "a wicked weed", this plant (pictured right) is still much used today. Can you identify it?

1 The characteristic flower shape of the trailing or climbing conservatory plant *Clianthus puniceus* (shown above) is responsible for what common name?

2 The majority of the 50 or so species of *Billbergia* (pictured left) are epiphytic. True or false?

3 A monopodial stem is one which continues to grow indefinitely from a single growing point, seldom or never branching. In which family of plants is this most usual?

4 *Livistona*, *Phoenix*, *Caryota* and *Howeia* all belong to which family of plants?
(a) Palms (b) Orchids (c) Ferns

5 During its winter rest period *Yucca aloifolia* or Spanish Bayonet, which has several variegated cultivars, should be watered in which of the following ways?
(a) Not at all (b) Sparingly (c) Plentifully

6 The climbing or trailing shrub *Hoya* or Wax Flower sheds its leaves in October or November. True or false?

7 What plant was popular with the Victorians, who gave it the name Cast-iron Plant for its ability to tolerate gas and smoke fumes, and was immortalized in a song?

8 The *Tradescantia* genus contains two species commonly known as Wandering Jew. One is *T. fluminensis*. The other, *T. pendula* (pictured right), was formerly listed under what other genus?

9 Which is the only one of the house plants listed below that prefers to be grown in shade?
(a) *Cineraria* (b) *Helxine* (c) *Gloxinia*

10 The leaves of the Peacock Plant, *Calathea makoyana*, are silvery green above and blotched with red or purple below, making it a much used foliage plant. From which country does it originate?
(a) India (b) China (c) Brazil

11 One commonly grown indoor species of *Primula* is *P. vulgaris*. What is the botanical name of the species that is often known as Fairy Primrose?

12 The pale green flowers of the epiphytic orchid *Brassavola nodosa* each have a white lip and give off a fragrance at night. By which of the following names is it more popularly known?
(a) Lady-of-the-night (b) Lady's Eardrops (c) Lady's Smock

1 This impressive tower (pictured left) looks down on the White Garden, the Nuttery, the Cottage Garden and the many other beautiful features of Sissinghurst Castle Gardens. After which famous 20th-century writer and garden designer is this tower named?

2 What word is applied to a row of balusters supporting a coping or parapet, a feature of many formal gardens?
(a) Belvedere (b) Palisade (c) Balustrade

3 Begun by the Holford family in 1829, Westonbirt Arboretum is the largest and oldest in Britain. What plants are grown in an arboretum?

4 Can you name the nurseryman and plantsman who pioneered the concept of island beds in the gardens of his Norfolk home?

5 Who played a prominent part in the development of the gardens at Hampton Court, and later forged a successful partnership with Henry Wise supplying large numbers of trees to gardens in many parts of the country?

6 This lawn mower (pictured right) is an early machine made by Ransome's of Ipswich, the company credited with producing the first factory-built, hand-propelled lawnmower. In what year was the first mower made?
(a) 1822 (b) 1832 (c) 1842

7 Leopold de Rothschild created a famous fruit collection at Gunnersbury House in London and later laid out a 12-hectare (30-acre) garden in Buckinghamshire with advice from Sir Harry Veitch, which included pools, rockeries and a topiary sundial. Where is this fascinating garden?

8 What name was given to the Victorian tool consisting of a flat rectangle of wood with a central handle set at an angle of 45 degrees, which was used for smoothing and weeding gravel walks?
(a) Beetle (b) Spider (c) Snake

9 Over 40 hectares (100 acres) of lavender (pictured above) can be seen at Caley Mill, Heacham, where the national collection of around 50 varieties is held. In which county is this collection?

10 The North Gardens at Sandringham are enclosed within lines of pleached limes and divided into sections by box hedges. Who designed them?

11 Which respected French painter created a pictorial record of the rose collection amassed at Malmaison by the Empress Josephine?

12 The shrub *Hypericum* 'Hidcote' is named after Hidcote Manor Garden in Gloucestershire. Which American created these gardens earlier this century?

ROUND EIGHTEEN

The spring-flowering perennial *Primula* or
Polyanthus, seen here growing with hyacinths,
is a garden hybrid thought to be derived from
the Wild Primrose. It is a plant that is often
increased by division, a process that should be
carried out immediately after the plant has
flowered. True or false?

1 *Rodgersia pinnata* (pictured above), which is grown for its foliage and flowers, originates from China. In Britain is it best planted in a dry, sunny position or moist shade?

2 Modern garden dahlias are derived from three species originating in which country?
(a) Chile (b) Mexico (c) Brazil

3 What name is given to a flat-topped cluster of flowers, the stalks of which arise one above the other from a vertical stem or axis, as in the Heliotrope?
(a) Corymb (b) Corolla (c) Corona

4 *Osmunda*, *Adiantum* and *Dryopteris* are all which type of plants?
(a) Grasses (b) Cacti
(c) Ferns

5 *Linum* (shown left) has more than 200 species of hardy and tender annuals, biennials, herbaceous perennials and sub-shrubs suitable for rock gardens and as pot plants for the conservatory. How is the genus better known?

6 One of around 600 species that make up the genus *Centaurea*, grown for their thistle-like flowers, is native to this country. The pigment from its blue petals was used by artists. By what name is the genus more usually known?

7 The winter-flowering hellebores produce flowers in a variety of colours. What single colour are the blooms of the widely grown species *Helleborus niger*, commonly known as the Christmas Rose?

8 The first bulbs of the lily *Cardiocrinum giganteum* were dispatched to Britain from the Himalayas in 1852. How long on average does it take from sowing to production of the first flowers?
(a) Two years (b) Four years (c) Seven years

9 A genus of bulbs native to tropical and southern Africa, *Crocosmia* (pictured right) belongs to the same plant family as which one of the following genera?
(a) *Iris* (b) *Tulipa* (c) *Clivia*

10 The Kingcup or *Caltha* is a hardy perennial in the same family as the Buttercup, but by which other name is it known, reflecting its suitability as a marginal?

11 The hardy perennial species of *Veronica* or Speedwell should be planted in well-drained but water-retentive soil. Will they do better in full sun or deep shade?

12 The hardy perennial Globe Thistle has handsome, spherical flowers with a metallic lustre, which are often cut and dried for winter decoration. Is this plant's botanical name *Echinops* or *Echinopsis*?

1 In summer, when the pea-like pods of the *Laburnum* (shown right) are ripening, young children may be taken to hospital after eating the poisonous seeds. Despite this, it is one of the most popular trees, grown for its cascades of yellow flowers which give rise to what common name?

2 'Bagshot Ruby', 'Dawn's Delight' and 'Pink Pearl' are all hardy hybrid forms in which genus of shrubs and trees?
(a) *Rhododendron*
(b) *Camellia* (c) *Rosa*

3 The sub-shrub *Hibiscus*, which has showy but short-lived flowers, belongs to the same plant family as *Malva* and *Althaea*. By what common name is this family known?

4 'Mission Bells', 'Mrs Popple' and 'Princess Dollar' are all hybrid varieties of *Fuchsia* suitable for growing outdoors. True or false?

5 Native to China, the common name of *Salix babylonica* 'Tortuosa' is descriptive of its twisted branches and contorted leaves. What is it?
(a) Lion's-claw Willow (b) Dragon's-claw Willow
(c) Eagle's-claw Willow

6 *Carpenteria californica*, an evergreen, summer-flowering shrub that prefers to be grown against a wall, is the only species in its genus. What word is used to describe such single-species plants?

7 Native to the Arctic regions and the mountains of the northern hemisphere, the hardy evergreen shrub *Cassiope* is grown for its heath-like foliage and tiny, bell-shaped flowers. It makes an ideal subject for a bank or rock garden, but should it be planted in acid or alkaline soil?

8 What structure could be defined as the mature carpel or collection of carpels, which may be either dry or fleshy and which bears ripe seeds?

9 A tree is a woody plant with a well-defined stem or trunk and a head of branches above. What term is given to shrubs such as roses or fuchsias that have been pruned and trained in this form?

10 This genus contains 200 species of evergreen and deciduous flowering shrubs and woody climbers with tubular, often fragrant flowers. Its common name may be preceded by Goat-leaf, Japanese or Scarlet Trumpet to provide the names of three of its species. Give either the common name or the botanical name.

11 Shrubs of the genus *Elaeagnus*, grown for their vari-coloured leaves, may be either evergreen or deciduous. Which of these descriptions fits the grey-green species Oleaster?

12 On warm, sunny days or when the plant is disturbed, *Helichrysum italicum* (pictured right) gives off a fragrance evocative of which of the following?
(a) Oranges (b) Curry
(c) Onions

1 Generally grown under glass in Britain, 'Long Purple' and 'New York' are well-flavoured, purple varieties of Egg Plant (shown left). How is this vegetable more often labelled in the shops?

2 Which of these three varieties of fruit is the odd one out and why?
(a) 'Emerald Gem'
(b) 'Alicante' (c) 'Golden Sunrise'

3 The dark brown residue resulting from the final breakdown of compost is generally referred to as what?

4 The Common Almond makes an excellent ornamental tree but will only rarely produce good quality nuts in the British climate. To which diverse genus of mainly deciduous trees does it belong?

5 Sweetcorn (pictured right) sown in the more southerly counties of Britain in mid May could be ready for picking in late August or September. How many cobs should each plant produce?
(a) One or two (b) Three to five (c) Five to eight

6 At approximately what age will a fan-trained, acid cherry tree produce its first fruit?

7 Figs can be grown as bush trees in southern and western areas of Britain. Can you name what is probably the best bush variety of fig, producing pale green fruits ripening to near white, a characteristic reflected in its name?

8 The winter varieties of radish are not particularly popular and very few find their way into suppliers' catalogues. Which of the following is just such a winter-cropping variety?
(a) 'Scarlet Globe' (b) 'French Breakfast' (c) 'China Rose'

9 The common herb *Tanacetum parthenium* (shown right) is said to be effective in the treatment of migraine, chills and nervous headaches. How is it more generally known?

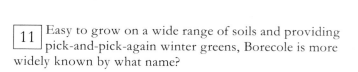

10 After the germination of the seeds, which of these minimum temperatures is it necessary to maintain in order to achieve a successful crop of melons?
(a) 18°C (64°F) (b) 16°C (61°F) (c) 11°C (50°F)

11 Easy to grow on a wide range of soils and providing pick-and-pick-again winter greens, Borecole is more widely known by what name?

12 'Green Hubbard', 'Butternut', 'Acorn' and 'Gold Nugget' are all forms of a vegetable belonging to the genus *Cucurbita* that is popular in its native America but still little used on this side of the Atlantic. What is it?

1 The graceful foliage plant *Dizygotheca elegantissima* (pictured right) was formerly included in another genus, a fact reflected in its common name. Which of the following is it?
(a) False Acacia (b) False Aralia (c) False Acanthus

2 Give the term applied to a temporary state of inactivity, usually in autumn and winter, when a plant makes little or no growth, its top growth (and sometimes, as with many bulbs, its roots) having withered away.

3 An insect on its leaf pad may activate trigger hairs causing two pads to close and the spine-like extensions to intermesh, after which the insect is chemically digested. What unusual house plant is being described?

4 The half-hardy, shrubby species and hybrids of Heliotrope may be used outdoors in a summer-bedding scheme. By what other common name is the genus *Heliotropium* sometimes known?
(a) Apple Pie (b) Pumpkin Pie (c) Cherry Pie

5 The unusually large, fragrant flowers of the *Echinopsis* each last for only a day or so although the plant remains in bloom for some time during the summer. Is *Echinopsis* an orchid, a cactus or a shrub?

6 The popular and charming annual house plant known by the common names Persian Violet, German Violet or Arabian Violet produces, as these names suggest, yellow-centred, fragrant, blue flowers. Can you give the botanical name of this plant?

7 Match the following plants with the countries of origin.
(i) *Crinum* (ii) *Cobaea* (iii) *Dipladenia*
(a) Mexico (b) Brazil (c) South Africa

8 The New Zealand shrub or small tree *Leptospermum* or Tea Tree produces a mass of bright, five-petalled flowers, but is this plant evergreen or deciduous?

9 *Allamanda cathartica* or Golden Trumpet, which is best displayed by providing the support of a trellis or cane, will produce its attractive golden-yellow blooms from March to June. True or false?

10 Which of the following house plants will not produce flowers in shades of red?
(a) *Syngonium* (c) *Callistemon*
(c) *Crossandra*

11 *Phoenix dactylifera* or Date Palm may be grown from the stones of Christmas dates but will only produce fruit if a male and female tree are grown in proximity to each other. True or false?

12 *Cereus peruvianus* (shown right) or Column Cactus is much admired as a conservatory plant for its sculptural, columnar shape. In the wild, however, what height will cacti of this genus frequently exceed?
(a) 9 metres (30 feet)
(b) 13.7 metres (45 feet)
(c) 18.3 metres (60 feet)

1 As a result of the importation of 40.6 tonnes (40 tons) of volcanic lava from Iceland by Joseph Banks, the first European habitat designed for rock plants was established in London in 1772. Where was it?
(a) Kew (b) Hampton Court (c) Chelsea Physic Garden

2 Which enthusiastic gardener and former Director of the Victoria and Albert Museum wrote *Creating Small Gardens* and *A Small Garden Designer's Handbook*?

3 What garden feature flourished in the 19th century inspired by the availability of material from far away countries and is usually asymmetrical in design, backed by a wall or hedge or standing alone as an island in the lawn?

4 Name the sub-tropical garden established in the northwest of Scotland by Osgood Mackenzie, Laird of Gairloch, in 1862 where, thanks to the Gulf Stream, New Zealand tree ferns, American pitcher plants and exotic bamboos all flourish outdoors.

5 What body dates back to the 14th century, received a Royal Charter in 1605, acted as a regulatory body for London's market gardens, and provided bridal bouquets for many royal marriages, including the Queen Mother's and that of the present queen?

6 Name the 16th-century barber-surgeon turned gardener (pictured left) who achieved fame after allegedly stealing the text and illustrations for his acclaimed *Herball*?

7 Though of uncertain origin, it has been claimed since the 19th century that the elevated topiary grouping (shown above) at Packwood House in Warwickshire represents which episode from the Bible?

8 Which celebrated Victorian naturalist wrote *The Fertilization of Orchids* in 1862 and *The Formation of Vegetable Mould through the Action of Worms* in 1881?

9 The Hampton Court International Flower Show has quickly achieved a truly international reputation since its inauguration in which of the following years?
(a) 1987 (b) 1990 (c) 1991

10 One of the many attractions in the grounds of Wallington House in Northumberland was created earlier in this century by Sir George and Lady Trevelyan and later modified by the National Trust. What is it?

11 During his 30-year partnership with Gertrude Jekyll he designed formal ground plans for hundreds of gardens, leaving Miss Jekyll a range of geometrical features to be softened by planting. Who was he?

12 Which Staffordshire gardens, now featuring a model railway and adventure playground, also boast a long lake landscaped by 'Capability' Brown and elegant terraces designed by Charles Barry?

ROUND NINETEEN

Created in the 1930s by Augustus Smith with considerable help from the warming influence of the Gulf Stream, these sub-tropical gardens in the Isles of Scilly are home to a host of exotic plants as well as many fine examples of landscaping, such as the Neptune Steps pictured here. Can you name these gardens?

1 'Rokesly Mini', 'Scarlet Comet' and 'Hamari Gold' are all modern hybrids of a popular flower that was discovered in Mexico by botanists travelling with the conquistadores. What is it?

2 The hardy perennial *Baptisia australis* (shown left) produces lupin-like spikes of bluish purple flowers followed by fat, dark grey seed pods. What is its common name?

3 *Rana temporaria* will help in some small measure to rid your garden of such pests as slugs, snails and greenfly. What is *Rana temporaria*?

4 The closely related plants *Tritonia*, *Ixia* and *Crocosmia* produce sword-shaped leaves and brilliantly coloured flowers. To which plant family do they all belong?

5 Which popular garden plant, said to have been cultivated in Japan for more than 2000 years, is that country's floral emblem?

6 The spring-flowering daffodil (pictured right) reproduces itself by producing smaller bulbs and may also be grown from seed. How would you increase this plant by vegetative propagation?

7 The spring-flowering *Viola* or pansy and *Bellis* or daisy are normally grown as biennials from seed sown the previous year. Which one of the following seasons is not an ideal time in which to sow the seed?
(a) Summer (b) Autumn (c) Spring

8 Taken from the name of a Greek goddess, this botanical term can be defined as the characteristic vegetation of an area. It is also used to describe a book in which this vegetation is listed and identified, such as the classic work on British plant life by the Reverend W. Keble Martin, first published in 1965. What is this term?

9 Sedge peat is generally black and is produced from rotting sedges. What do we call the generally browner material made from decaying mosses?

10 *Geum rivale* is ideal for the front of a border. What is its common name, which reflects its need for a moist soil?

11 With its fern-like foliage and creamy-white flowers, *Myrrhis odorata* (shown right) is similar in appearance to Cow Parsley. What is its common name?

12 The dwarf, shrubby succulent *Lampranthus*, which is closely related to the *Mesembryanthemum*, will grow rapidly in poor soil, but in which of the following situations is it likely to grow best?
(a) In shade (b) On a dry stone wall (c) Near water

1 Staff Vine and Climbing Bittersweet are both common names of a climbing shrub (pictured above) producing yellow-green flowers followed by pea-sized, brightly coloured ornamental fruit. What is its botanical name?

2 Which of the following is the common name of the bush *Rubus cockburnianus*, derived from the white bloom that covers its shoots?
(a) Snow Bramble (b) Whitewashed Bramble (c) Cloudy Bramble

3 With its closely packed branches and dwarf habit, *Juniperus communis* 'Compressa' is an ideal choice for the rockery. What is the shape of *J. virginiana* 'Skyrocket'?

4 Name the gas that plants extract from the air and convert into sugar?

5 What is the common name of this poplar (shown right), which is also the name of the region in northern Italy from which it was brought to Britain as a cutting in the 18th century.

6 *Miscanthus* originates in the orient and has varieties such as 'Silver Feather' and 'Zebrinus'. What kind of plant is *Miscanthus*?
(a) Fern (b) Bamboo (c) Grass

7 'Handsworth New Silver', 'J.C. van Tol', and the yellow-berried 'Bacciflava' are all varieties of which plant?

8 The most commonly planted ornamental willow is the Golden Weeping Willow, which is often grown by ponds. It spreads by means of long-haired, wind-borne seeds, produced in late summer. True or false?

9 Although more than a thousand species and varieties of conifers are now grown in British gardens, only three of these are native plants. The Common Juniper and the Yew are two. The third (pictured right) is the most widespread of all pines. Can you name it?

10 *Abutilon vitifolium* has oval, sharply toothed, grey-green leaves and produces masses of bowl-shaped blooms from late spring to early summer. What colour are these flowers?

11 *Cotoneaster* is a genus containing about 50 species of dwarf, creeping shrubs or small deciduous trees, which can be grown in partial shade. True or false?

12 Most species of *Pittosporum* are native to Australasia but what is the country of origin of *P. tobira*, which has dark green leaves and heavily scented flowers?
(a) Brazil (b) Nepal (c) Japan

1 The herb *Artemisia dracunculus* or Little Dragon (shown right) is most commonly used to flavour vinegars. How is it more popularly known?

2 According to historical records which fruit has been in cultivation longer than any other?

3 What pest do gardeners hope to deter by soaking their Broad Beans in paraffin before sowing?

4 In 1990 V. Throup of Silsden, West Yorkshire, set a new world record for the heaviest onion. At which of the following weights did the record breaker tip the scales?
(a) 4.93 kilograms (10 pounds 14 ounces) (b) 5 kilograms (11 pounds) (c) 6.1 kilograms (13 pounds 7 ounces)

5 What is the name of the portable covers of glass or plastic (pictured left) which are available in various sizes and are now mainly used for raising early crops in the open?

6 The ornamental Turban Gourd and Bottle Gourd belong to the family Cucurbitaceae. What is the name of the popular fruit belonging to the same family that has the varieties 'Ringleader' and 'Tiger'?

7 Having grown varieties such as 'Meteor', 'Kelvedon Wonder', 'Improved Pilot' and 'Pioneer', which part of the plant would you eat?
(a) Swollen root (b) Seeds (c) Leaves

8 The fruit bush varieties 'Bluecrop' and 'Spartan' should be pruned between November and March and will only thrive in acid soil. What fruit will they produce?

9 The Channel Island of Jersey produces potatoes that are popular throughout Britain. For which fruit is the neighbouring island of Guernsey famous?

10 The salad plant *Montia perfoliata* or Winter Purslane (shown above) acquired another common name from its use by Californian gold miners as a source of greens in spring. What is this name?

11 Two of the three varieties named below are raspberries. Which is the odd one out, in that it is an apple?
(a) 'Malling Admiral' (b) 'Glen Moy' (c) 'Malling Kent'

12 All varieties of peach and nectarine bear their delicious fruit on shoots that are produced the previous year. True or false?

1 During its flowering period, the *Neoregelia* undergoes a striking change as the leaf tips and the central rosette turn bright red. At what time of year does this happen?
(a) Summer (b) Autumn (c) Any time

2 What name is given to the small, barbed, bristly hairs that are found, sometimes in tufts, on cacti such as *Opuntias* (pictured right)?

3 The sub-shrub *Ruellia macrantha* needs a humid atmosphere and a minimum temperature of around 15°C (60°F) to produce its funnel-shaped flowers. What is its country of origin?

4 The mat-forming, green-leaved *Soleirolia soleirolii* or Mind Your Own Business has stems that root as they grow. Under which other genus may this plant be listed?

5 What term describes a leaf or petal that has wavy or slightly crimped margins, as in *Asplenium nidus*?
(a) Pinnate (b) Undulate (c) Obovate

6 Which exotic conservatory and house plant, with spectacular orange and blue flowers and paddle-shaped leaves, takes its scientific name from the family name of George III's bride, Queen Charlotte?

7 Despite its palm-like appearance, *Beaucarnea recurvata* is actually a member of the agave family of succulents. Which of the following is not one of its common names?
(a) Fan Plant (b) Ponytail Plant (c) Elephant's-foot Plant

8 The house plants *Fatsia japonica* (shown right), *Syngonium* and *Rhoicissus* can all tolerate situations with relatively low light. True or false?

9 If a yucca grows too tall for its position, the trunk or stem may be cut down in spring and new growth will soon appear from the top. True or false?

10 The common name of the succulent *Pachyphytum oviferum*, a relative of the *Echeveria*, results from the powdery bloom covering its grey-blue foliage. What is it?

11 The process by which plants continually lose water from their stems and leaves varies greatly from one species to another, and with the time of day or year. What is this process called?

12 Best grown in a conservatory except in the mildest areas, the evergreen climber *Jasminum mesnyi* (pictured below) bears unscented flowers in spring. Is it commonly known as Primula Jasmine or Primrose Jasmine?

1 | The Brizlee Tower at Alnwick, the Gothic Tower at Pains Hill (shown above) and Alfred's Tower at Stourhead are all fine examples of which of the following?
(a) Belvedere (b) Shot tower (c) Pagoda

2 | Captain Cook's first landfall in Australia was at a place he originally called Stingray Bay. Cook later renamed the area Botany Bay in recognition of the work of a famous naturalist and plant collector. Who was this?

3 | Founded by the brothers Thomas and Daniel Hanbury in the 19th century, on a sheltered Italian promontory, this botanical garden was claimed by one admirer to form 'the principal collection of living plants in the world'. Can you supply its name?

4 | What is the name of the 16-hectare (40-acre) strip of landscaped grounds on both sides of the river Cam in Cambridgeshire, stretching from St John's College in the north to Queen's College in the south.

5 | Haddon Hall, Hardwick Hall and Keddlestone Hall all boast impressive gardens. In which English county can these three halls be found?
(a) Staffordshire (b) Cheshire (c) Derbyshire

6 | Having achieved celebrity in his native France, which landscape architect designed or greatly influenced both St James' Park and Kensington Gardens in London?

7 | Which plant, named after an 18th-century French botanist, is the floral emblem and part of the popular name of the American state of Mississippi?

8 | In the gardens of which house in Saffron Walden, Essex, would you find a 'Capability' Brown lake crossed by a Robert Adam bridge, as well as the Elysian Gardens designed by Richard Wood?

9 | The resident scientist on *Gardeners' Question Time* is currently Dr Stefan Buczacki. Who preceded him in this position, joining the panel in 1950?

10 | Which botanist and plant collector became the first Director of the Royal Botanic Gardens, Kew, in 1841?

11 | The Victorian passion for ironmongery led to a variety of tools for very specific jobs. Which garden implement might have been French, ring-lock or scissor-action (pictured right)?

12 | The gardener and architect Joseph Paxton is remembered for his work at Chatsworth and the Crystal Palace, but to which of these posts was he elected in 1854?
(a) Lord Mayor of London
(b) MP for Coventry
(c) Director of Kew Gardens

ROUND TWENTY

Perennial anemones flower at varying times of the year. The majestic and graceful *Anemone hybrida* or Japanese Anemone shown here produces its loose clusters of white, pink or red blooms in late summer and autumn, and is ideal for a border. From which of the following does it grow?
(a) Corm (b) Tuber (c) Fibrous root

1 *Allium porrum* is to Wales as *Onopordum acanthium* is to which other country?

2 The perennial *Francoa sonchifolia* (shown left), which bears pink, bell-shaped flowers on graceful stems from summer to autumn, is ideal as a pot plant for a sunny patio. What is its common name? (a) Wedding Bells (b) Bridal Wreath (c) Happy Ever After

3 Which garden bulb, once considered difficult to grow in Britain but now widely cultivated for its spectacular, six-petalled, scented flowers, contains the species *davidii*, *martagon* and *auratum*, and the varieties 'Enchantment', 'Imperial Crimson' and 'Journey's End'?

4 With its distinctive, funnel-shaped flowers, whose petals each have a prominent spur, the Columbine is a delightful addition to the herbaceous border. What is its botanical name?

5 Most plants are dicotyledons, meaning that the first leaves produced by the seeds are in pairs. What is the most common monocotyledon?

6 The attractive Alpine Snowbell (pictured right) makes an ideal plant for the rock garden. To what genus does it belong?

7 Strawberry Blite bears ornamental fruit, and Chop-suey Greens and Ice Plant produce decorative flowers, but for what practical purpose may these plants be worth growing other than as attractive additions to the garden?

8 Which half-hardy plant, grown mainly for summer bedding, produces flower heads of fluffy clusters resembling shaving brushes and has popular forms called 'Fairy Pink' and the long-flowering F_1 hybrid 'Blue Chip'?

9 The *Arctotis*, which originates in the Americas, has large, bright flowers that tend to close in the afternoon and during overcast weather. How are they best described? (a) Snapdragon-like (b) Daisy-like (c) Poppy-like

10 *Caltha palustris* (shown right) is a spring-flowering hardy perennial suitable for growing at the edge of a pond. What is its common name, part of which reflects this preferred location?

11 The annual *Gilia*, with its attractive, deeply divided, fern-like foliage, and showy flowers of varying shapes and colours, thrives in a well-drained, sunny spot. From which of these American states does it originate? (a) Arizona (b) California (c) Texas

12 The summer-bedding plant *Salvia splendens*, which has densely packed, red flower spikes, belongs to the largest genus in the family Labiatae. This genus contains about 900 species. True or false?

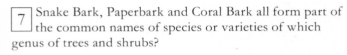

1 The deciduous *Leycesteria formosa* (pictured right) produces long racemes of claret bracts on tall, bamboo-like stems, followed, in autumn, by berries much favoured by Blackbirds. What colour are these berries?
(a) Creamy white
(b) Orangey red
(c) Purplish black

2 To enable the twiggy evergreen shrub *Andromeda* to thrive and produce its pitcher-shaped, pink or white flowers in spring or early summer, should it be planted in acid or alkaline soil?

3 Trees belonging to the genus *Platanus* are usually grown for their attractively lobed and toothed leaves and flaking bark, although they do produce inconspicuous flowers and, in autumn, spherical fruit clusters. By what name are these trees more commonly known?

4 *Cornus nuttalli* (shown left), which has large, white bracts, was first identified in California by David Douglas in the 1820s. How is the genus *Cornus* better known?

5 'Golden Wonder', 'Pembury Blue' and 'Boulevard' are all pyramidal forms of which popular conifer?
(a) Cypress (b) Juniper (c) Yew

6 The species *Lapageria rosea*, *Embothrium coccineum* and *Berberis linearifolia* were all introduced into Britain from China. True or false?

7 Snake Bark, Paperbark and Coral Bark all form part of the common names of species or varieties of which genus of trees and shrubs?

8 The bushy shrub *Grindelia chiloensis* produces sticky, lance-shaped leaves and, in summer, large, daisy-like flowers. What colour are these flowers?
(a) Yellow (b) White (c) Pink

9 'Adam', 'Emerald Globe', 'Glacier' and 'Tricolor' are all forms of which widely grown evergreen climber?

10 The dozen or so deciduous conifers of the genus *Larix* (pictured right), originating in temperate northern regions, are suitable as specimen trees. How are they more generally known?

11 The species *Salix lanata*, *Santolina chamaecyparissus* and *Hippophae rhamnoides* all bear leaves of which colour?
(a) Deep purple (b) Pale yellow (c) Silver-grey

12 The dense, bushy evergreen shrub *Sarcococca* has small, dark green leaves, and produces tiny, white, fragrant flowers in winter. What is its common name?

121

1 *Vaccinium oxycoccos* bears globular or pear-shaped red berries (shown left) in August and September. These are sometimes used in pies or drinks, but are best known as the basis of a sauce served with turkey at Thanksgiving in the United States. How are these fruits commonly known?

2 Which of the following causes the roots of plants to grow downwards?
(a) Magnetism (b) Gravity (c) Light sensitivity

3 Common, Blue and Cockspur are common names of animals whose value to gardeners was first demonstrated by Charles Darwin in an 1881 publication. What are they.

4 *Anthriscus cerefolium* (pictured right), a herb with hollow, aromatic stems and green, ferny leaves similar to those of Parsley, is used for flavouring salads, soups and sauces. What is its common name?

5 The leaves of a marrow become puckered and mottled yellow, light and dark green, while the fruits are also mottled and reduced in size. Which disease, whose name suggests it is more at home on another vegetable, is the most likely cause?

6 In 1991 Thompson and Morgan introduced the new variety 'Icarus', claimed to be tastier and richer in vitamin C. What type of fruit or vegetable is 'Icarus'?

7 Although it is sometimes listed as Italian Broccoli, 'Romanesco' is in fact a variety of which other type of vegetable?

8 Which little-known leguminous annual (shown left), whose name suggests a relationship to another vegetable, bears scarlet flowers and crinkly, green, edible seed pods?

9 Giant tomatoes such as 'Ponderosa' and 'Oxheart' are known in America as Beefsteak Tomatoes. What name is given to the giants produced in Italy and Spain?

10 Can you name the device (pictured right) that was used to water fruit and vegetables before the advent of the high-pressure hose?

11 Which fruit is borne by the self-fertilizing varieties 'Amsden June', 'Peregrine' and 'Rochester'?

12 Which one of the following vegetables is not usually grouped under the general heading of *Brassicas*?
(a) Brussels Sprouts (b) Kale (c) Celeriac

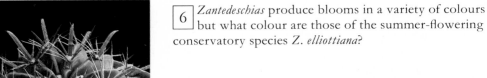

1 The common name of the *Ferocactus* (shown right) is derived from its spherical shape, although it will in time become columnar. What is its common name?
(a) Cotton-reel Cactus
(b) Barrel Cactus
(c) Globe Cactus

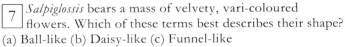

2 An excellent house plant may be produced by suspending the stone from the fruit of *Persea americana* over a tumbler of water with the broadest end just in contact with the surface. By what name is this fruit better known?

3 The popular climber *Thunbergia alata* or Black-eyed Susan is a native of South Africa. What is the country of origin of its relative *T. grandiflora*, which produces pale, purple-blue flowers?
(a) China (b) India (c) Brazil

4 What is the approximate minimum temperature required by *Hibiscus rosa-sinensis* to ensure that it retains its foliage throughout the winter?
(a) 10°C (50°F) (b) 15°C (60°F) (c) 20°C (70°F)

5 A useful source of winter colour, the popular conservatory or house plant *Azalea indica* (pictured left) bears a profusion of red, white or pink blooms. In order to thrive, this plant needs a cool, humid environment and permanently moist compost. True or false?

6 *Zantedeschias* produce blooms in a variety of colours but what colour are those of the summer-flowering conservatory species *Z. elliottiana*?

7 *Salpiglossis* bears a mass of velvety, vari-coloured flowers. Which of these terms best describes their shape?
(a) Ball-like (b) Daisy-like (c) Funnel-like

8 Once widely used as an orchid-growing medium, the material known as *Osmunda* fibre is produced from the dried roots of which plant?

9 One of the smallest but most unusual of the bromeliads, *Tillandsia* (shown right) bears a pink flower spike that produces its blue-violet flowers at almost any time of year. Which of these names does not apply to this plant?
(a) Pink Quill
(b) Blue-flowered Torch
(c) Violet Flame

10 A Poinsettia grown on from the previous year will only produce its attractive flower bracts if, from mid September onwards, it is exposed to a strict lighting regime of 10 hours of light a day. True or false?

11 What is the common, fishy-sounding name of the American plant *Columnea*, which is often grown as a basket plant for its showy, hooded flowers?

12 What name is given to the sticky, sugary substance that deforms the growth of many house plants after it has been excreted by greenfly, whitefly, scale insects and mealybugs in the process of feeding?

1 The predecessor of the modern-day 'window-in-the-wall' (shown above) consisted of a wrought-iron screen set into garden walls to extend the view. What was it called?
(a) Trompe l'oeil (b) Clair-voyée (c) Exedra

2 Of which 18th-century landscape gardener did the writer Horace Walpole say "He leaped the fence and saw all nature was a garden."?
(a) Humphry Repton (b) Charles Bridgeman
(c) William Kent

3 The tree *Chamaecyparis lawsoniana* or Lawson's Cypress was first identified on the west coast of America in the mid 19th century by the eponymous Mr Lawson. What was his occupation?
(a) Botanist (b) Nurseryman (c) Physician

4 Name the mathematician, navigator and soldier who colonized the Falkland Islands for France and who is commemorated in the name of a genus of tropical, scrambling climbers with showy floral bracts?

5 Which 17th-century poet, satirist, pamphleteer and Member of Parliament, a friend and collaborator of John Milton, wrote the famous poem 'The Garden'?

6 Which of the following gardens is not situated in the county of Kent?
(a) Knole (b) Hidcote Manor (c) Hever Castle

7 In 1929 Thomas Mawson became the first president and Brenda Colvin, Sylvia Crowe and Geoffrey Jellicoe founder members of which institute?

8 Unearthed by the German Robert Koldewey at the start of the 20th century, they were created for Queen Amytis some 2500 years earlier. What are they?

9 What is the name of the artificial lake in Surrey, completed in 1782, which forms part of the southern boundary to Windsor Great Park?

10 The tropical conservatory that was opened in 1987 is the largest of all the greenhouses at Kew Gardens. After which member of the Royal Family is it named?

11 Can you name the political association formed in honour of Benjamin Disraeli and still in existence today, which includes the name of a spring-flowering plant, thought to be his favourite?

12 This traveller (shown right), naturalist and head gardener to Charles I established in Lambeth, London, the first public museum, which later formed the basis of the Ashmolean Museum in Oxford. Can you name him?

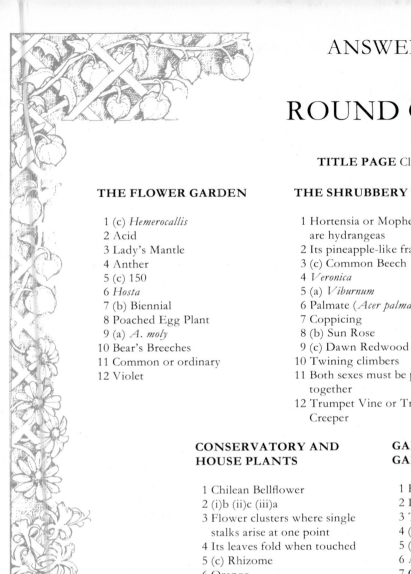

ANSWERS

ROUND ONE

TITLE PAGE Cliveden

THE FLOWER GARDEN

1 (c) *Hemerocallis*
2 Acid
3 Lady's Mantle
4 Anther
5 (c) 150
6 *Hosta*
7 (b) Biennial
8 Poached Egg Plant
9 (a) *A. moly*
10 Bear's Breeches
11 Common or ordinary
12 Violet

THE SHRUBBERY

1 Hortensia or Mophead; they are hydrangeas
2 Its pineapple-like fragrance
3 (c) Common Beech
4 *Veronica*
5 (a) *Viburnum*
6 Palmate (*Acer palmatum*)
7 Coppicing
8 (b) Sun Rose
9 (c) Dawn Redwood
10 Twining climbers
11 Both sexes must be planted together
12 Trumpet Vine or Trumpet Creeper

THE KITCHEN GARDEN

1 Curly-leafed Kale
2 (c) 'Grenadier'
3 Apricot
4 Peach-leaf Curl
5 Production will stop
6 Leek
7 Scion
8 (b) 'Blue Lake'
9 Chocolate Spot
10 (i)b (ii)a (iii)c
11 (b) Four years
12 Angelica

CONSERVATORY AND HOUSE PLANTS

1 Chilean Bellflower
2 (i)b (ii)c (iii)a
3 Flower clusters where single stalks arise at one point
4 Its leaves fold when touched
5 (c) Rhizome
6 Orange
7 Tiger Orchid
8 *Rhipsalidopsis* has flat stems; *Schlumbergera* has rounded
9 Deer's Foot Fern, Stag's Horn Fern
10 (b) *Ficus pumila*
11 *Kentia*
12 Hot-water Plant

GARDENS AND GARDENERS

1 Holkham Hall
2 Lawn mower
3 The Alhambra
4 (i)b (ii)c (iii)a
5 (a) Decimus Burton
6 African Violet
7 Crinkle-crankle
8 Hatfield House
9 Derry and Toms
10 Wardian case
11 Claude Monet
12 (c) St Albans

ROUND TWO

TITLE PAGE Flowers

THE FLOWER GARDEN

1 Blue
2 Herbaceous
3 Seedling
4 *Colchicum*
5 False; it is evergreen
6 Moist conditions
7 (b) Jacob's Ladder
8 False; Phlox is American
9 Candytuft
10 (a) Saxifrage
11 Bright sunlight
12 Castor-oil Plant

THE SHRUBBERY

1 Crepe Myrtle
2 False; flowers in spring
3 (a) Honey Locust
4 Late autumn to early winter
5 Virginia Creeper
6 Stolons
7 Judas Tree
8 Red
9 (a) Junipers
10 Lemon Verbena
11 False; it needs lime-free
   soil
12 White

THE KITCHEN GARDEN

1 *Salvia*
2 False; friable
3 Turnip, swede, radish
4 Kiwi Fruit or Chinese
   Gooseberry
5 Chicory
6 (b) Globe Artichoke
7 Black
8 Lamb's Lettuce
9 Strawberry
10 'Greyhound'
11 Pomegranate
12 April or May

CONSERVATORY AND HOUSE PLANTS

1 *Lantana*
2 Southern USA to South
   America
3 (c) King of Hearts
4 At ground level
5 (b) Bromeliads
6 Cactus
7 Bleeding Heart Vine
8 (c) Blue
9 (b) Wait-and-see
10 (b) *Opuntia*
11 Norfolk Island Pine
12 (i)b (ii)c (iii)a

GARDENS AND GARDENERS

1 Wisley
2 (c) Shropshire
3 Coconut fibre
4 (a) Ferns
5 (a) Ebbw Vale
6 Ness Gardens
7 Lutyens bench
8 Norman Painting – Phil
   Archer of *The Archers*
9 Biddulph Grange,
   Staffordshire
10 Nicholas Culpeper
11 Topiary
12 Clay Jones

ANSWERS

ROUND THREE

TITLE PAGE Leopard's Bane

THE FLOWER GARDEN

1 (a) Spring
2 False; fleshy tuberous roots
3 (c) Love-lies-bleeding
4 Axil
5 (a) Partly shaded and moist
6 Dibber or dibble
7 (a) Europe
8 Evening Primrose
9 True
10 *Malcolmia*
11 *Pulsatilla*
12 Sport or chimera

THE SHRUBBERY

1 (c) Mediterranean
2 Hip
3 (c) Smoke Bush
4 False; it needs an acid soil
5 *Sorbus*
6 Yellow
7 *Calluna*
8 *Eucalyptus*
9 *Rhododendron*
10 Aspen
11 Spindle
12 *Forsythia*

THE KITCHEN GARDEN

1 *Citrus*
2 Brussels Sprouts
3 Potato Cyst Eelworm
4 Basil
5 Currants
6 (b) 'Tender and True' is a parsnip; the others are onions
7 Loofah
8 Strawberry
9 Carrot
10 Oxalic acid
11 Globe Artichoke
12 Kohl-rabi

CONSERVATORY AND HOUSE PLANTS

1 False; pink only
2 False; autumn
3 Scarborough Lily
4 (a) Sparingly
5 Succulents
6 Yellow Jasmine is a rambler; White Jasmine is a climber
7 Swiss Cheese Plant
8 *Bougainvillea*
9 True
10 Mexico
11 Tender Broom
12 Prayer Plant

GARDENS AND GARDENERS

1 Levens Hall
2 Blenheim
3 Tea production
4 Queen Victoria
5 (b) Obelisk
6 Neo-Italianate
7 Peter Beales
8 (b) The National Gardens Scheme
9 Vita Sackville-West and Harold Nicolson
10 Alton Towers
11 Bodnant
12 Humphry Repton

ANSWERS

ROUND FOUR

TITLE PAGE Treated as an annual

THE FLOWER GARDEN

1 (b) South Africa
2 Chrysanthemum
3 Beautiful
4 Division
5 Chinese Lantern
6 Corm
7 *Nerine bowdenii*
8 Tilth
9 Wild Hyacinth
10 Marigold
11 *Rheum palmatum*
12 (b) Summer Snowdrop

THE SHRUBBERY

1 White
2 Divided into several pairs of oppositely arranged leaflets
3 (b) *Kalmia*
4 *Buddleia*
5 Bushy
6 Snake-bark Maple
7 (c) *Euphorbia*
8 *Pendula*
9 *Rhododendron*
10 Green above and white below
11 (Pocket) Handkerchief Tree
12 Wisteria

THE KITCHEN GARDEN

1 Fennel
2 Sweet cherry
3 Grafting
4 (b) Cobnut
5 (i)a (ii)c (iii)b
6 Apple
7 Long-rooted
8 Potato
9 Pumpkin
10 Carrot Fly
11 *Pyrus communis*
12 (a) 'Giant White'

CONSERVATORY AND HOUSE PLANTS

1 Indian Shot Plant
2 (b) India
3 Bract
4 (c) Plentifully
5 *Cyperus*
6 (a) *Phalaenopsis*
7 Bellflower
8 *Spathiphyllum*
9 Hydroponics
10 False (it climbs or trails)
11 (c) Cup-and-saucer Vine
12 Australia

GARDENS AND GARDENERS

1 Myrtle
2 (b) Michel Begon
3 (b) 1913
4 Potpourri
5 Sir William Chambers
6 (c) Flower painter
7 Rosemary Verey
8 Anne Boleyn
9 The National Trust
10 Lindisfarne or Holy Island
11 Copenhagen
12 Knot garden

ANSWERS

ROUND FIVE

TITLE PAGE (c) Fairhaven

THE FLOWER GARDEN

1 Autumn
2 Reflexed
3 (b) *Calendula*
4 Thorn Apple
5 Leguminosae
6 Sea Kale
7 Burning Bush
8 *Gladiolus*
9 True
10 Coneflower
11 (c) *Scilla*
12 (a) Daisy-like

THE SHRUBBERY

1 Seed
2 Aluminium sulphate
3 Chilean Glory Flower
4 i(c) ii(a) iii(b)
5 (c) Mount Etna Broom
6 (b) Pines
7 Beauty Bush or *Kolkwitzia amabilis*
8 Vermouth or absinthe
9 (c); it is deciduous
10 (b) New Zealand
11 Privet
12 *Fuchsia*

THE KITCHEN GARDEN

1 Parsley or *Petroselinum crispum*
2 Silver Leaf
3 *Capsicum* or Sweet Pepper
4 (b); it needs moist, acid soil
5 Onion
6 (b) Pumpkin
7 (c) Hazel
8 They are all red
9 Coriander
10 May and June
11 Walking sticks
12 (c); they grow best in acid soil

CONSERVATORY AND HOUSE PLANTS

1 (c) 18°C (65°F)
2 Hen-and-chicken Fern
3 (b) *Clerodendrum*
4 Princess Flower or Glory Bush
5 (b) *Adiantum*
6 False; it has insignificant flowers
7 (a) Pocket Flower
8 Mexican Firecracker
9 White
10 (b) *Gardenia*
11 *Tolmiea menziesii*
12 (c) Succulents

GARDENS AND GARDENERS

1 Dovecote
2 (a) Bicton
3 (b) Otto Brunfels (*Brunfelsia*)
4 (b) Holland
5 Père Armand David
6 Peter Seabrook
7 Roses
8 E. A. Bowles
9 (c) West Sussex
10 Marianne North
11 (a) Malaysia
12 (c) Scottish

ANSWERS

ROUND SIX

TITLE PAGE *Clematis viticella*

THE FLOWER GARDEN

1 (c) China
2 An increase in acidity
3 (c) *Lavatera* is European
4 (b) Cuttings
5 (b) Drumstick Primula
6 (c) Candlewicks
7 Cranesbill
8 Culm
9 Stratification
10 *Delphinium*
11 Bright yellow
12 False; permanently moist soil

THE SHRUBBERY

1 *Camellia*
2 Haw
3 Adam's Needle
4 It peels to reveal a different colour underneath
5 Crab Apple or Flowering Crab
6 *Ceanothus*
7 False; cut back to the second or third bud
8 Twisted
9 Pruning
10 (b) Holly
11 North America
12 *T. baccata* 'Elegantissima'

THE KITCHEN GARDEN

1 Seville Orange
2 Common growth forms
3 Cucumber
4 (c) 'Denniston's Superb' is a plum; the others are apples
5 Borage
6 Jerusalem Artichoke
7 Cauliflower
8 Kale
9 Melon
10 (c) 'Lloyd George' is a raspberry
11 Long-rooted
12 False; 'Red Knight' is a stick variety

CONSERVATORY AND HOUSE PLANTS

1 Mother-in-law('s Tongue)
2 False; each is a related but separate genus
3 Epiphyte or epiphytic
4 South America
5 White
6 (c) Palms
7 Yesterday-today-and-tomorrow
8 Tree Fern
9 Edible
10 (b) Rose of Jericho; it is a *Hibiscus*
11 (a) Cactus
12 (c) Scape

GARDENS AND GARDENERS

1 (b) Laburnum walk
2 *Tapis vert*
3 Alton Towers pagoda
4 Percy Thrower
5 (b) Sandringham
6 Hampton Court
7 Pergola
8 (c) William Kent
9 (a) Bees
10 Roy Lancaster
11 Joseph Paxton
12 (b) East Sussex

ANSWERS

ROUND SEVEN

TITLE PAGE Rembrandt and Parrot

THE FLOWER GARDEN

1 Summer
2 Campion
3 *Dianthus*
4 Pinching out or stopping
5 (b) Great Britain
6 Snuff
7 Moist
8 *Ajuga reptans*
9 *Trillium*
10 Fleshy root
11 (a) Dutch Hyacinth
12 *Tanacetum*

THE SHRUBBERY

1 Scandent
2 Late autumn to early spring
3 Catkin
4 Cladodes
5 True
6 (b) Silk Tassel Bush
7 Russian Vine
8 True
9 Triangular
10 Evergreen
11 (c) 30 years
12 Mistletoe

THE KITCHEN GARDEN

1 Leatherjackets
2 Varieties of apple
3 Loquat
4 (a) Apple (b) Gooseberry (c) Rhubarb
5 White
6 Gooseberry ('The Gooseberry Growers' Anthem')
7 Self-heal
8 Pear
9 True
10 Sweetcorn
11 Marrow
12 Forcing Sea Kale and rhubarb

CONSERVATORY AND HOUSE PLANTS

1 (c) African Hemp
2 Latex
3 Blood Lily
4 True
5 Lime-free
6 *Kalanchoe*
7 (i)c (ii)a (iii)b
8 It is the only one
9 False; it needs to be well-lit
10 Rhizome
11 Orchids
12 (b) *Schizanthus*

GARDENS AND GARDENERS

1 Newby Hall
2 Shirley Hibberd
3 (a) Brittany
4 Topiary
5 Terracotta pot
6 Geoffrey Smith
7 Lord Byron
8 Lady Amherst
9 McIntosh's Patent
10 Mount Stewart
11 Ruin
12 (c) Sir Walter Raleigh (the potato)

ROUND EIGHT

TITLE PAGE The Pantheon

THE FLOWER GARDEN

1 False; it requires full sun
2 Double-flowered
3 (b) Tuber
4 Tobacco
5 Hollyhock
6 Edelweiss
7 (a) Floret
8 Every three or four years
9 Spit
10 (b) *Primula*
11 *Monarda*
12 Gentian

THE SHRUBBERY

1 Norway Spruce
2 (c) Australasia
3 Pollarding
4 (c) Bamboo
5 (b) *Rhus*
6 Cedar of Lebanon
7 *Santolina*
8 (c) Golden Rain Tree
9 All yellow leaves
10 (b) *Fremontodendron*
11 Sea-green
12 Deciduous

THE KITCHEN GARDEN

1 (b) 'Brown Turkey'
2 Pear
3 Nectarine
4 *F.v. dulce*
5 Mangetout
6 Chicons
7 Broccoli or Calabrese
8 Chives
9 Celeriac
10 Tap root; it is horseradish
11 Layering
12 Salsify

CONSERVATORY AND HOUSE PLANTS

1 Orchid
2 Easter Cactus
3 False; it grows from a corm
4 Short-lasting
5 (c) Prayer Plant
6 *Plumbago*
7 Rosette
8 It is a climber
9 (c) *Howea*
10 Air plants
11 *Clivia*
12 (c) 50 years

GARDENS AND GARDENERS

1 Ventnor
2 Douglas Fir
3 William Wordsworth
4 Pinetum
5 (a) Posy
6 National Garden Centre
7 (c) Queen Caroline
8 Hans Sloane
9 Long Barn
10 (a) Swedish
11 (b) Maggiore
12 Carolus Linnaeus (Carl Linné)

ANSWERS

ROUND NINE

TITLE PAGE Spores

THE FLOWER GARDEN

1 False; 400
2 (c) Hybrid
3 Madonna Lily
4 July
5 Sweet William
6 Heel
7 (c) Kansas
8 Scarifying
9 *Gladiolus*
10 True
11 pH 7
12 Rhizome

THE SHRUBBERY

1 (c) Climbing
2 (a) Portugal
3 (a) Prostrate
4 *Ginkgo biloba*
5 Acorns
6 Fragrant
7 Elm
8 (a) Bamboo
9 Before
10 Sucker
11 *Magnolia grandiflora*
12 *Salix*

THE KITCHEN GARDEN

1 Marjoram
2 Fork or rake; it's a prong
3 (c) 'Big Boy'
4 Snails
5 True
6 Apple Sawfly
7 (c) 23.9 kilograms (52 pounds 12 ounces)
8 Leaf Beet or Swiss Chard
9 True
10 *P. crispum* is a herb while *P.c. tuberosum* is a root vegetable
11 (c) 'Whinham's Industry' is a gooseberry; the others are strawberries
12 Stellate fan

CONSERVATORY AND HOUSE PLANTS

1 Like the head of a lance
2 Dragon Tree
3 (c) 13°C (55°F)
4 False; they need low humidity
5 (c) *Canna*
6 Cape Primrose
7 True
8 Yellow
9 False; it is a foliage house plant
10 (a) Christ Plant
11 Kangaroo Vine
12 Cycadaceae

GARDENS AND GARDENERS

1 Gertrude Jekyll
2 Trellis-work
3 Chatsworth
4 (a) Maze
5 John Tradescant the Younger
6 (b) Parson
7 National Association of Flower Arrangement Societies
8 (a) 4 hectares (10 acres)
9 Hampshire
10 (c) Avenue
11 The Orangery
12 Arley Hall

ANSWERS

ROUND TEN

TITLE PAGE (b) Thomas Archer

THE FLOWER GARDEN

1 (a) Balloon Flower
2 (c) 'Treneague'
3 (c) Australia
4 Dead-heading
5 Yellow
6 True
7 Dandelion (*dent de lion*)
8 Chincherinchee
9 Valerian
10 *Brunnera*
11 (c) 'George Harrison'
12 Rocket; *Eruca vesicaria sativa* is Rocket and *Hesperis matronalis* is Sweet Rocket

THE SHRUBBERY

1 Indian Bean Tree
2 Bud
3 Yellow
4 Acid soil
5 Rue or Herb of Grace
6 Persian Ironwood
7 *Phillyrea*
8 Periwinkle
9 Elder
10 No
11 Feather Grass
12 (a) Red

THE KITCHEN GARDEN

1 (c) 12 months
2 Garden spade
3 Parsnip
4 Rosemary
5 Swollen stem
6 Whiptail
7 Summer Squash
8 Cloves
9 November to December
10 *Scorzonera*
11 Self-fertile
12 September or October

CONSERVATORY AND HOUSE PLANTS

1 Pineapple Lily
2 Late spring to early summer
3 Plunging
4 *Begonia*
5 Orange
6 Brazil
7 (c) Goldfinger Cactus
8 South America
9 False; it is winter-flowering
10 (a) *Zantedeschia*
11 (c) *Hypoestes*
12 Cactus

GARDENS AND GARDENERS

1 Studley Royal
2 (b) Arran
3 (b) 1850
4 Rose
5 Thomas Rochford
6 (a) Walled kitchen garden
7 (b) Oxford Botanic Gardens
8 John Claudius Loudon
9 (c) Flower arranging
10 Wakehurst Place
11 George Forrest
12 Reginald Farrer

ROUND ELEVEN

TITLE PAGE *Rhododendron*

THE FLOWER GARDEN

1 *Mimulus*
2 Marginal
3 True
4 (c) Spiderwort
5 (i)b (ii)c (iii)a
6 Useful to people
7 (c) 400
8 Grafting, cuttings, layering, division, budding
9 Stamen
10 Queen; Queen's Tears, Queen Anne's Jonquil
11 False; Turkey and Kashmir
12 Snapdragon or *Antirrhinum*

THE SHRUBBERY

1 *Ribes sanguinium*
2 China
3 False; prune during February
4 True
5 Whorl
6 Gorse
7 (c) 1894
8 (b) Twining climber
9 Gymnosperms
10 Ivy
11 Witch Hazel
12 True; it is Walnut – native to southeastern Europe, China and the Himalayas

THE KITCHEN GARDEN

1 Runners or stolons
2 (Swiss) Chard
3 Runner, French and Broad
4 Cane
5 Tomato
6 Thyme
7 Espalier
8 Lettuce
9 Grafting
10 Giant Puffball
11 Blanching
12 (b) June to October

CONSERVATORY AND HOUSE PLANTS

1 *Gynura*
2 False; India or Africa
3 Pseudobulb
4 *Begonia*
5 To increase humidity
6 Blooms open in the morning, fading by evening
7 They are carnivorous
8 *Hippeastrum*
9 (a) Deep shade
10 Lollipop Plant
11 Prickly Pear
12 True

GARDENS AND GARDENERS

1 Royal Botanic Gardens, Edinburgh
2 (b) 140
3 Empress Josephine of France
4 Sir Francis Dashwood
5 True
6 (c) Boskett (a formal thicket of trees)
7 Joseph Dalton Hooker
8 Castle Howard
9 Joseph Banks
10 (b) Lincolnshire
11 George Russell
12 Ernest 'Chinese' Wilson

ROUND TWELVE

TITLE PAGE Dwarf Fan Palm

THE FLOWER GARDEN

1 *Godetia*
2 Hardening off
3 False; it is a tuber
4 Buttercup
5 (a) Early spring
6 (b) Cabbage
7 After
8 Teasel
9 Blue
10 (b) Snapdragon-like
11 (a) *Tiarella*
12 (b) Woolly

THE SHRUBBERY

1 True
2 Tree-like
3 (a) Daisy Bush
4 Parasite or parasitic
5 Monkey Puzzle
6 'Veitchii' is female and
   needs a male form
7 White
8 Mulberry
9 Shrub
10 Acid
11 (a) Heather
12 (b) March

THE KITCHEN GARDEN

1 Bay
2 Green manuring
3 False; they are dwarf forms
4 Berry
5 Leek
6 Mint
7 (c) 4.9 metres (16 feet)
8 Hand lights
9 Turnip
10 Banana
11 Ladies' Fingers
12 Loganberry

CONSERVATORY AND HOUSE PLANTS

1 They act as parachutes
2 (b) Orchid Tree
3 Mildew
4 (b) Fiddle-leaf Fig
5 Australia
6 True (Agavaceae)
7 (b) Cigar Flower
8 True
9 *Crassula*
10 (c) Late winter
11 The finely toothed edges are
   very sharp
12 (b) Multi-coloured

GARDENS AND GARDENERS

1 Powis Castle
2 Lancelot
3 (b) Channel Islands
4 (b) Clusius (Charles de
   l'Ecluse)
5 (c) John McRae
6 Thomas Rivers of
   Sawbridgeworth
7 David Stevens
8 Windsor Great Park
9 Frank Kingdon-Ward
10 Armillary sphere
11 Herbaceous border
12 John Evelyn

ANSWERS

ROUND THIRTEEN

TITLE PAGE Scree

THE FLOWER GARDEN

1 False; late spring to early summer
2 Petunia
3 Catmint
4 Node
5 (b) Hart's-tongue Fern
6 (a) *Heleborus*
7 (c) *Kalmia*
8 Bulb
9 *Saxifraga*
10 *Viola odorata* or Sweet Violet
11 *Iris reticulata*
12 Coasts

THE SHRUBBERY

1 Peaches, plums, almonds, apricots
2 Bole
3 True
4 *Robinia*
5 Grasses
6 Chinese
7 (c) 90 metres (99 yards)
8 *Thuja*
9 Beech
10 (c) Mexico
11 *Mahonia × media* 'Charity'
12 (a) *Spiraea*

THE KITCHEN GARDEN

1 Saffron
2 (c) 'Dutch Yellow' is a shallot; others are onions
3 Swedes
4 Curd
5 Damson
6 *Capsicum* species
7 Make it bitter
8 Kent
9 Leek, garlic, shallot
10 Cabbage Root Fly
11 Root
12 Mallow or Malvaceae

CONSERVATORY AND HOUSE PLANTS

1 *Abutilon*
2 Joseph's Coat
3 Red or pink (*rubescens* means 'blushing')
4 Aerial roots
5 (b) Winter Cherry
6 Cacti
7 (b) Variegated
8 (a) Mediterranean
9 Angel; Angel's Wing, Angel's Tears, Angel's Trumpet
10 (c) *Cineraria*
11 Living Stones
12 Flamingo (Flower)

GARDENS AND GARDENERS

1 Gwynedd
2 Carpet bedding
3 Anglesey Abbey
4 John Innes
5 Stove house
6 (b) William Kerr (*Kerria*)
7 Robert Adam
8 John Bartram
9 André le Nôtre
10 True
11 (b) William Robinson
12 (a) Palisade

ROUND FOURTEEN

TITLE PAGE Immediately after flowering

THE FLOWER GARDEN

1 False; Mediterranean region
2 *Anemone*
3 (c) White
4 *Lobelia*
5 Thrift or Sea Pink
6 True
7 Evergreen
8 (c) *Polygonatum*
9 Alpine plant
10 *Bellis*
11 Royal blue
12 (a) *Primula*

THE SHRUBBERY

1 New Zealand
2 (c) Oak
3 Eglantine
4 Tendril
5 True
6 Lime
7 False; April and May
8 Yellow
9 Japan
10 *Rubus* includes all three
11 Conkers
12 *Artemisia*

THE KITCHEN GARDEN

1 Hyssop
2 Chlorosis
3 (b) Raspberry
4 Yellow
5 True
6 Pickling
7 Pineapples
8 (b) 'Czar'
9 Endive
10 Lemon Balm
11 Nut
12 Kohl-rabi

CONSERVATORY AND HOUSE PLANTS

1 (b) South Africa
2 Umbrella Plant or Umbrella Tree
3 Dumb Cane
4 Mid winter
5 *Fatshedera* (*Fatsia* and *Hedera*)
6 False; 16°C (61°F) is enough
7 Purple
8 True
9 Desert Privet
10 Pitcher plants
11 (b) *Callisia*
12 *Kalanchoe*

GARDENS AND GARDENERS

1 Waddesdon Manor
2 Alan Titchmarsh
3 Limestone rock garden
4 Garden bower
5 Madeira
6 (c) County Down
7 True
8 Mathias de L'Obel (*Lobelia*)
9 Jane Loudon
10 Treillage
11 Rose
12 Harlow Car Gardens

ANSWERS

ROUND FIFTEEN

TITLE PAGE *Pieris*

THE FLOWER GARDEN

1 (b) Spathe
2 Monocarpic
3 Dog-tooth Violet
4 Nectar
5 (b) *Fuchsia*
6 Michaelmas Daisy
7 New Zealand
8 Perennial
9 (i)a (ii)b (iii)c
10 False; Golden Rod
11 King Protea
12 *Statice*

THE SHRUBBERY

1 (c) Winter Jasmine
2 Upright or column-like
3 Tap root
4 *Viburnum*
5 Scots Pine
6 Layering
7 Box
8 North America
9 (a) Rose
10 *Escallonia*
11 Ash
12 Quince

THE KITCHEN GARDEN

1 Tuber
2 (b) 'Grandee' is a strawberry
3 Cordon
4 Zucchini (which is also the Italian name)
5 Caraway
6 Quince
7 False; 16°C (61°F)
8 Cabbage
9 (i)a (ii)c (iii)b
10 Sweet Pepper or *Capsicum*
11 Medlar
12 (c) 'The Prince' is a bean; the others are beetroots

CONSERVATORY AND HOUSE PLANTS

1 *Datura*
2 Black-eyed Susan
3 (c) *Jacaranda*
4 (c) Deciduous
5 *Areca lutescens*
6 *Pot-et-fleur*
7 *Gardenia*
8 (a) Grass-like
9 True
10 False; Parlour Palm
11 True
12 Fronds

GARDENS AND GARDENERS

1 Devon
2 (b) 1804
3 (b) County Down
4 Versailles planter
5 Dorset
6 John Vanbrugh
7 (b) Battering
8 Beth Chatto
9 (c) Stowe
10 Capability Brown
11 The Great Conservatory, Chatsworth
12 Robert Fortune

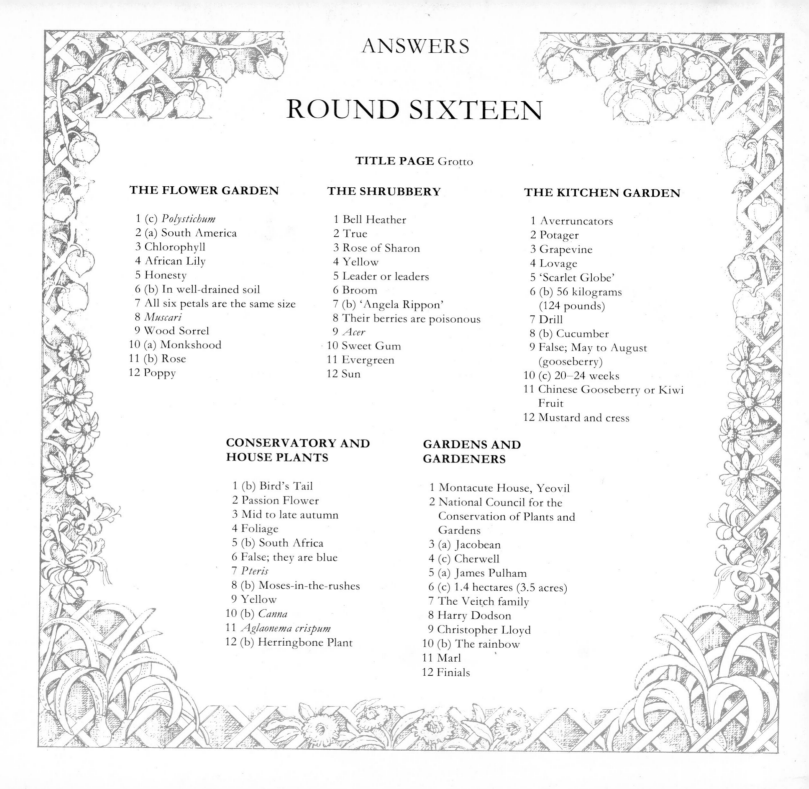

ANSWERS

ROUND SIXTEEN

TITLE PAGE Grotto

THE FLOWER GARDEN

1 (c) *Polystichum*
2 (a) South America
3 Chlorophyll
4 African Lily
5 Honesty
6 (b) In well-drained soil
7 All six petals are the same size
8 *Muscari*
9 Wood Sorrel
10 (a) Monkshood
11 (b) Rose
12 Poppy

THE SHRUBBERY

1 Bell Heather
2 True
3 Rose of Sharon
4 Yellow
5 Leader or leaders
6 Broom
7 (b) 'Angela Rippon'
8 Their berries are poisonous
9 *Acer*
10 Sweet Gum
11 Evergreen
12 Sun

THE KITCHEN GARDEN

1 Averruncators
2 Potager
3 Grapevine
4 Lovage
5 'Scarlet Globe'
6 (b) 56 kilograms
   (124 pounds)
7 Drill
8 (b) Cucumber
9 False; May to August
   (gooseberry)
10 (c) 20–24 weeks
11 Chinese Gooseberry or Kiwi
   Fruit
12 Mustard and cress

CONSERVATORY AND HOUSE PLANTS

1 (b) Bird's Tail
2 Passion Flower
3 Mid to late autumn
4 Foliage
5 (b) South Africa
6 False; they are blue
7 *Pteris*
8 (b) Moses-in-the-rushes
9 Yellow
10 (b) *Canna*
11 *Aglaonema crispum*
12 (b) Herringbone Plant

GARDENS AND GARDENERS

1 Montacute House, Yeovil
2 National Council for the
  Conservation of Plants and
  Gardens
3 (a) Jacobean
4 (c) Cherwell
5 (a) James Pulham
6 (c) 1.4 hectares (3.5 acres)
7 The Veitch family
8 Harry Dodson
9 Christopher Lloyd
10 (b) The rainbow
11 Marl
12 Finials

INSTANT FIRST AID IN VERSE

See to his breathing, look at his face
Seek for the Pulse with fingers in place.
Look for Deformity, swelling or stain
If patient recovers, ask where he feels pain.

The face may be flushed, pale, ashen or blue
Look for symptoms; signs; decide what to do.
Asphyzia's urgent you must treat this first
And next in importance, a blood vessel that's burst.

Should the patient be restless, gasping and dry
There's Haemorrhage there, unseen to the eye.
Wrap him in blankets, and let him have air
His condition is serious, treat him with care.

If fracture is suspected, examine, make sure
With splint, pad and bandage, make it secure.
And if there is damage to Pelvis or back,
Lift him with coat, blanket or sack.

APROX — check

borus orientalis (Mar – May) ●

~~llearanus~~ foetidus (Nov – Feb) e/g

Monarda (beebalm) (June – July)

Ligularia dentata `Desdemona`

~~Sea~~ Sedum spectabile (now Hylotelephium
spectabile)

Geranium (Cranesbill)

~~Stachys lanata~~ e/g

Nepeta

Aster (July – Sept +)

Kniphofia (late Summer / early Aut)

Ajuga (late sp)

Heuchera (Spring)

Clematis recta [border herbaceous]

Anemone [hardy herbaceous]

~~Tut~~

ROUND SEVENTEEN

TITLE PAGE *Trichodiadema*

THE FLOWER GARDEN

1 *Meconopsis betonicifolia* or Himalayan Blue Poppy
2 (a) South America (Peruvian Lily)
3 Digitalis
4 (c) Peltate
5 Tulip
6 (b) *Ipomoea* (500 species)
7 Mulch
8 True
9 *Viola*
10 Nasturtium
11 True
12 (c) *Dianthus*

THE SHRUBBERY

1 True
2 Topiary
3 False; they need sun or dappled shade
4 Mock Orange
5 *Daphne*
6 Poplar
7 Lilac
8 Keys
9 Yellow
10 (a) China
11 Golden
12 Sub-shrubs

THE KITCHEN GARDEN

1 (b); should be below 120 metres (400 feet)
2 Asparagus
3 Clamp
4 Brussels Sprouts
5 False; 'Morello' is an acid cherry
6 Gooseberries
7 Codling Moths
8 Carrot
9 Spinach
10 (b) 18th
11 Loganberry
12 Hop or *Humulus*

CONSERVATORY AND HOUSE PLANTS

1 Parrot's Bill
2 True
3 Orchids
4 (a) Palms
5 (b) Sparingly
6 False; it is evergreen
7 *Aspidistra*
8 *Zebrina*
9 (b) *Helxine*
10 (c) Brazil
11 *Primula malacoides*
12 (a) Lady-of-the-night

GARDENS AND GARDENERS

1 Vita Sackville-West (Vita's Tower)
2 (c) Balustrade
3 Trees
4 Alan Bloom
5 George London
6 (b) 1832
7 Ascott
8 (a) Beetle
9 Norfolk
10 Sir Geoffrey Jellicoe
11 Pierre Joseph Redouté
12 Major Lawrence Johnston

ROUND EIGHTEEN

TITLE PAGE True

THE FLOWER GARDEN

1 Moist shade
2 (b) Mexico
3 (a) Corymb
4 (c) Ferns
5 Flax
6 Cornflower
7 White
8 (c) Seven years
9 (a) *Iris*
10 Marsh Marigold
11 Full sun
12 *Echinops*

THE SHRUBBERY

1 Golden Rain Tree or Golden Chain
2 (a) *Rhododendron*
3 Mallow
4 True
5 (b) Dragon's-claw Willow
6 Monotypic
7 Acid
8 Fruit
9 Standard
10 Honeysuckle or *Lonicera*
11 Deciduous
12 (b) Curry

THE KITCHEN GARDEN

1 Aubergine
2 (a) 'Emerald Gem' is a melon; the other two are tomatoes
3 Humus
4 *Prunus*
5 (a) One or two
6 Three to four years
7 'White Marseilles'
8 (c) 'China Rose'
9 Feverfew or Featherfew
10 (b) 16°C (61°F)
11 Kale
12 Pumpkin or Winter Squash

CONSERVATORY AND HOUSE PLANTS

1 (b) False Aralia
2 Dormancy
3 Venus Fly Trap
4 (c) Cherry Pie
5 Cactus
6 *Exacum*
7 (i)c (ii)a (iii)b
8 Evergreen
9 False; July to September
10 (a) *Syngonium*
11 True
12 (a) 9 metres (30 feet)

GARDENS AND GARDENERS

1 (c) Chelsea Physic Garden
2 Sir Roy Strong
3 Shrubbery
4 Inverewe
5 The Worshipful Company of Gardeners
6 John Gerard
7 The Sermon on the Mount
8 Charles Darwin
9 (b) 1990
10 Secret walled garden
11 Sir Edwin Lutyens
12 Trentham Gardens

ANSWERS

ROUND NINETEEN

TITLE PAGE Tresco Abbey Gardens

THE FLOWER GARDEN

1 Dahlia
2 False Indigo
3 Common Frog
4 Iris or Iridaceae
5 Chrysanthemum
6 Cutting the bulb into pieces ('chipping')
7 (a) Summer
8 Flora
9 *Sphagnum* peat
10 Water Avens
11 Sweet Cicely
12 (b) On a dry stone wall

THE SHRUBBERY

1 *Celastrus*
2 (b) Whitewashed Bramble
3 Tall, upright and narrow
4 Carbon dioxide
5 Lombardy Poplar
6 (c) Grass
7 Holly or *Ilex aquifolium*
8 False; it is a sterile hybrid, grown from cuttings
9 Scots Pine
10 Purplish-blue
11 True
12 (c) Japan

THE KITCHEN GARDEN

1 French Tarragon
2 Apple
3 Mice
4 (a) 4.93 kilograms (10 pounds 14 ounces)
5 Cloches
6 Melon
7 (b) Seeds; they are peas
8 Blueberries
9 Tomatoes
10 Miners' Lettuce
11 (c) 'Malling Kent'
12 True

CONSERVATORY AND HOUSE PLANTS

1 (c) Any time
2 Glochids
3 Brazil
4 *Helxine*
5 (b) Undulate
6 *Strelitzia reginae* (Duchess of Mecklenberg-Strelitz)
7 (a) Fan Plant
8 True
9 True
10 Sugared Almond Plum
11 Transpiration
12 Primrose Jasmine

GARDENS AND GARDENERS

1 (a) Belvedere
2 Sir Joseph Banks
3 La Mortola
4 The Backs
5 (c) Derbyshire
6 André Le Nôtre
7 Magnolia State (Pierre Magnol)
8 Audley End House
9 Dr (later Professor) Alan Gemmell
10 Sir William Hooker
11 Transplanter
12 (b) MP for Coventry

ROUND TWENTY

TITLE PAGE (c) Fibrous root

THE FLOWER GARDEN

1 Scotland; it is a thistle, the country's floral emblem
2 (b) Bridal Wreath
3 Lily
4 *Aquilegia*
5 Grass
6 *Soldanella*
7 They are all edible
8 *Ageratum*
9 (b) Daisy-like
10 Marsh Marigold
11 (b) California
12 True

THE SHRUBBERY

1 (c) Purplish black
2 Acid soil
3 Plane
4 Dogwood
5 (a) Cypress
6 False; Chile
7 *Acer* or Maple
8 (a) Yellow
9 *Hedera helix* or Common Ivy
10 Larch
11 (c) Silver-grey
12 Christmas Box

THE KITCHEN GARDEN

1 Cranberry
2 (b) Gravity
3 Earthworms
4 Chervil
5 Cucumber Mosaic Virus
6 Brussels Sprouts
7 Cauliflower
8 Asparagus Pea
9 Marmandes
10 Garden or water engine
11 Peach
12 (c) Celeriac

CONSERVATORY AND HOUSE PLANTS

1 (b) Barrel Cactus
2 Avocado Pear
3 (b) India
4 (b) 15°C (60°F)
5 True
6 Yellow
7 (c) Funnel-like
8 *Osmunda regalis*; a fern
9 (c) Violet Flame
10 True
11 Goldfish Plant
12 Honeydew

GARDENS AND GARDENERS

1 (b) Clair-voyée
2 (c) William Kent
3 (b) Nurseryman
4 Louis Antoine de Bougainville
5 Andrew Marvell
6 (b) Hidcote Manor (Gloucestershire)
7 The Institute of Landscape Architects
8 The Hanging Gardens of Babylon
9 Virginia Water
10 The Princess of Wales
11 The Primrose League
12 John Tradescant the elder